Praise for
When Everything Changed

Dr. Sheri cannot be classified. She is more of a "force" than an individual, moving people to better health and optimism with her own story, her inspiring words, and her endless dedication to living life joyfully regardless of circumstance.

Tanya Abreu, Founder & Chief Vision Officer, Spirit of Women Hospital Network and international expert on the business of women's health

Dr. Sheri's book exemplifies triumph over tragedy and re-minds me that we all have unimaginable power and strength inside of us. While this is one amazing woman's story, her words cause reflection to moments in our own lives where we learn life simply is not always fair, but what matters most, as Dr. Sheri eloquently lays out to us, is what we should do next—in a word, L.I.V.E.!

Carlissa Crawford, SPHR, MHRM, Executive HR Consultant

Dr. Sheri has a true passion and gift for helping women live their best life despite obstacles. Her personal journey makes her most qualified to lead women through what could be the most difficult time in their lives. Her test to not let her obstacles define her or slow her down has truly become her testimony!!!

Karyn Greer, Anchor, NBC Affiliate, Atlanta

Dr. Sheri continues to be a great example of how one can survive a life-changing, potentially life-destroying illness and redirect the force of that tragedy to recreate her life's mission in a way that inspires everyone who meets her. At a time in her life when everything should have finally settled into familiar patterns, she figured out how to tackle the worst head on. Her story will motivate you to make the most of the life you have been given.

Jacqueline Walker, MD

Dr. Sheri has transcended her battle with cancer and become a source of love and inspiration to thousands for women and men still navigating their own journey with the disease. She makes the world a better place.

Norm Bowling, Chief Revenue & Marketing Officer, Susan G. Komen

Dr. Sheri has the ability to motivate the human spirit into a higher level of existence with her words. Her gift is undeniable and it is abundantly clear that the higher power is using her in a mighty way! Dr. Sheri uses her personal journey to illustrate that we can all rise above our circumstances, reinvent ourselves, and learn to live in our purpose!

Egypt Sherrod, TV Host & Entrepreneur

Sheri is one of the strongest people I have ever known. She simply can't be summed up in a few sentences or even a few chapters. She is the epitome of inspiration. I could go on about how she's turned life's lemons into lemonade or found the silver lining behind the dark cloud, but it doesn't do her justice. She just rocks.

Mauna Pandya, MD, Medical Oncologist

When
Everything
Changed

My Journey from Physician to Patient

Dr. Sheri Prentiss

Edited by
Janice Williams Miller

WHEN EVERYTHING CHANGED
MY JOURNEY FROM PHYSICIAN TO PATIENT

Cover image courtesy of American College of Physician Executives.

iUniverse books may be ordered through booksellers, author's website at www.drsherimd.com or by contacting:

iUniverse
1663 Liberty Drive
Bloomington, IN 47403
www.iuniverse.com
1-800-Authors (1-800-288-4677)

Because of the dynamic nature of the Internet, any web addresses or links contained in this book may have changed since publication and may no longer be valid. The views expressed in this work are solely those of the author and do not necessarily reflect the views of the publisher, and the publisher hereby disclaims any responsibility for them.

ISBN: 978-1-4917-4834-3 (sc)
ISBN: 978-1-4917-4835-0 (e)

Library of Congress Control Number: 2014918994

Printed in the United States of America.

iUniverse rev. date: 10/22/2014

Dedication

In loving memory of my mom, Yvonne Springs. No one will ever love me like you. You've gone on to be with the Lord in Heaven, and yet daily I live to make you proud.

Contents

Preface

In 2011 I set out to write my story of how the tragedies of cancer, death, disability, and divorce forced me to L.I.V.E., which is trademarked and part of my signature.

> Love myself and others
> Inspire those around me
> Voice my dreams and ambitions
> Enjoy life

I wanted to expose my raw feelings to people who found themselves in my shoes and who could relate to what I felt so that they might find strength to live also. I figured my unique perspective of sympathetic outsider turned empathetic insider would be valuable.

This project was grueling. It was overwhelming at some points of the process. I kept thinking about the tens of thousands of women I had met, most of whom were between the ages of 25 and 50. They were also overwhelmed when life's demands—marriage, graduate school, career choices, childbearing, divorce, retirement planning, empty nesting, care of parents—met tragedy. The sheer weight of it all had made it easy to relinquish power to painful situations, fear, misperceptions, or people.

This book demonstrates my discovery that to LIVE means to struggle with what we have rather than what we've lost. My hope is that my putting pen to paper (or fingers to keys) helps women breathe new life into dying hope.

Introduction

When Everything Changed holds the revelations I learned along my journey from physician to patient. It presents answers to the questions that flooded me during that transition: Can I survive breast cancer without treatment? Is there life, health, and happiness after cancer? How can I live with the death of my mother while in the throes of despair from my own tragedy?

In the early stages of my terrifying diagnosis, I wanted to die. Not just give up. Die! I was in unchartered territory. Up to that point, outside of the run-of-the-mill life challenges, I had soared. My mother had done everything in her power to make sure of it. Her charter for me at 30,000 feet, though, was to carry others with me. Sure enough, when one tragedy after another hit, they were watching. I had to get this right to maximize the outcome of my influence on their lives. I had no permission to quit. As unfair as that sounds and counter to the self-preservation narrative, I was fortunate. Through my struggle to live, for me and for them, I learned the truth of the matter. The truth about self. The truth about others. It is this valuable information that you will find in the pages that follow.

None of us was made for easy, but with an enormous power within our frailty. From behind our fear emerges our courage; from beyond our defeat boasts our victory; and on the heels of our struggles strut our triumphs, manifesting our dreams and visions.

I am Dr. Sheri, and my prescription for life is to L.I.V.E.

Love myself and others
Inspire those around me
Voice my dreams and ambitions
Enjoy life

1

Mom's Girl

The day my mom and I began making arrangements for her impending homegoing, I began losing a part of myself. She was both "mom" and "girlfriend," depending on who I needed her to be. We would shop and cook together, comb each other's hair, and share hours of girl talk. For every milestone in my life, she was right there front and center.

Mom was the first to respond when, at the age of two during an episode of *Marcus Welby, MD*, I gallantly stood on my parents' bed and announced that I wanted to be a doctor. "Baby, you will make a great doctor! Why do you want to become a doctor?" she asked. I replied, "Because I want to help people aaannd make a lot of money!"

When the struggle became her own, she proved to me that there was always a way and a reason to smile.

Mom cracked up laughing, not because she disbelieved her innocent toddler's words or their plausibility. She was delighted that she was raising yet another brutally honest child.

From that moment on Mom supported me in everything that led to becoming a doctor. She attended every parent-teacher conference and awards assembly. She'd come home after a full day's work, cook, and still somehow find the time to help me polish a creative writing assignment or to clarify a point on my personal statement for my college applications.

One thing Mom didn't have to do too often for me was tend to the sick. Either I would soak in her at-the-ready remedies of soup, juice, and Vick's VapoRub or ignore my symptoms completely, because I despised missing school. I felt like all the other kids would be ahead of me. So when the mumps and chicken pox struck, my mom spent more time consoling me over the loss of school days than taking care of my ailments.

Once when I was a junior in high school, I avoided mentioning that I had shortness of breath, chest tightness, headache, and fatigue for a week. On this particular day, getting to school was frightening. It felt like I had lead in my shoes and all of my classmates were gliding quickly past me. I stopped by my guidance counselor's office for my routine college, extracurricular, or personal chat, but the look of horror on her face said it all. I dug my heels in deeper. *I made it to school, and, darn it, I'm going to every class and earn my perfect attendance award.*

When she asked how I was feeling, I replied, "I'm okay." In my head, though, my voice sounded more like a dying robot who had just gotten the wires pulled out of its back.

I then meekly asked, "Can I call my mom?"

When my mother answered the phone, I began, "If I need you to come and pick me up, can you do it?"

Her two word response was, "Of course."

To this day I don't know how she left her job downtown on public transportation to go an hour south to our home to get the car and then drive northwest to my school in less than an hour.

For the next five days that I lay in bed, she waited on me hand and foot. She arranged for my friends to bring my homework home daily so I wouldn't freak out, preparing special treats for their trouble. She even wielded her charm, wit, and drop dead gorgeous smile to get my attendance record cleaned for the semester.

Childhood stories like this abound about the woman who taught me to love hard. She didn't just feel sorry for struggling people. She was driven by empathy to help them by any means necessary. When the struggle became her own, she proved to me that there was always a way and a reason to smile.

Mom had been sick on and off for years while I was in college. She had asthma and bronchitis, or so we were told. After I had become a resident, she suffered a bout of bronchitis during which her doctor noticed a "granulomatous lesion resembling tuberculosis" on her lung. I told her to request a sarcoidosis work up, and two weeks later the results confirmed my suspicion. Naturally, there were absolutely no diagnostic tests, treatment options, or decisions made without my approval.

Sarcoidosis, rarely, could be deadly. In some people, symptoms would begin suddenly and/or severely and subside in a short period of time. Others would have no outward symptoms. Still others' symptoms would appear slowly and subtly but last or recur over a long time span. My mom's case fell into that last category. Most common among middle-aged, African-American women, there was no cure. The most we could do was medicate to maintain the proper working order of the lungs. So, in true diva style, my mom went all out, taking just about every medication known to treat it.

After 10 years of sarcoidosis scarring her lungs, Mom needed oxygen support. Within months she went from needing two liters of oxygen with moderate physical activity to about six liters at rest. It quickly became clear that without a bilateral lung transplant she would die. So, again in true diva fashion, we spent tens of thousands of dollars and hundreds of hours testing and waiting for results. Finally, a renowned transplant team at one of the best teaching hospitals in Chicago told us the devastating news. She was not a candidate. Her lungs were too scarred for her to live through the operation. We brought her home, and she and I began planning her homegoing.

After five excruciating months of planning, I decided to take a break and throw myself a 40th birthday bash at my house with close friends and family. Through the December 12, 2007 blizzard and my pleading with her to stay home and rest, my mom appeared, oxygen in tow and laboring for every breath.

She said that only death would keep her from spending that day with me. Her death was my greatest fear.

Mom didn't seem to be sharing my fear, though. She was still enjoying life. Though weak and sick she would shout, "Wait!" every time someone snapped a picture with her in it. She wanted time to pull the oxygen cannula out of her nose! How I loved that vain woman.

2
The Big "C"

By June 3, 2008 Barack Obama had secured enough delegates to become the presumptive nominee of the Democratic Party for the 2008 presidential election. Half the country was in anticipation, but I was in trepidation. *Are my children at risk for sarcoidosis? How much should I share with them? What more can I do for Mom?*

Mom was declining, so I went into caregiver overdrive, which I learned from the best. I ramped up my routine. After a 10–12 hour work day, I'd come home to take care of my two teenage daughters. Then, I'd go to laugh and reminisce with Mom for hours in the room I had designed and decorated especially for her. I'd keep her favorite snacks nearby and treat her to hand, foot, and scalp massages until she fell

October 1, 2008, my life changed forever. I didn't get married, didn't have a baby, and didn't get a new job. I found a lump in my right breast.

asleep. On occasion I brought her to my home for a "spa getaway."

The strain of my mom's impending death had taken its toll. I had no appetite, I couldn't sleep, and I had a hard time focusing. I was totally drained, losing the strength to hold her, lacking the will to let her go. I tried to encourage myself: *Sheri, you can do this. You're as ready as you will ever be. You'll have great memories to comfort you.*

On October 1, 2008, my life changed forever. I didn't get married, didn't have a baby, and didn't get a new job. I found a lump in my right breast. Normally, I would have run to tell my mother, but I was frozen by my discovery. I knew it was cancer from the moment I felt it, because no one knows my body better than I do. I decided not to tell her until I received confirmation.

A moment later, my mother called. She had made it to St. James, an inpatient hospice just minutes from my house where we could best manage her medications and comfort. This would be the last time she would go.

Two days later, after a diagnostic mammogram and ultrasound, I rushed to see her, knowing she was in her last days. Immediately, she noticed my hospital ID bracelet. I had forgotten to remove it. She graciously let me blow off her inquiry with, "Just my doctors running some tests."

Over the course of the following week, the doctors sent Mom home from hospice with sufficient medication to see her comfortably into the kingdom. The week they sent her home was the same week the doctors officially diagnosed me with "invasive ductal carcinoma of the right breast."

I had spent the last three years helping Mom prepare to die. I had even told her that I was ready for her to go, as ready as her youngest could ever be, but everything had changed. I was no longer ready to accept that she would die. I needed her so desperately.

For two years she had repeatedly asked God why was He keeping her alive. When I told her my diagnosis, one of the hardest things I've ever done, she said, "Now I know why I'm still here. Even though I can't be much help to you, a baby needs her mommy when she gets a diagnosis like that." With that, she resolved to live as long as necessary.

October 22, 2008 was a day of no significance to millions of people around the globe, but for me it was the day I lost half of my right breast in a partial mastectomy. My surgeon had hoped that my lesion was benign and that my sentinel node biopsy would be negative, but she had to go in four times, cutting more and more cancerous tissue out of my breast. The moment she felt my sentinel node between her fingers, the truth struck her like a ton of bricks, and she began the lymph node dissection.

Much to my dismay, I awoke from surgery to the news that three out of 16 nodes were positive. My surgeon stood at the side of my bed with plenty tears and few words. I held her hand and told her we would talk in the morning.

The next day, I woke to a tube draining excess

blood and fluid from my right arm pit. The day before I had anticipated going home after a few hours with, worse case, a few radiation treatments to follow. How drastically my life had changed in less than 24 hours! I lay pondering how I would add chemotherapy and radiation to my routine. My childhood resistance to being sick had persisted.

On the evening of November 4, 2008, Election Day, I watched as the world celebrated a turn in history. Barack Obama was elected the first African-American President of the United States of America. I saw the smiles and I heard the shouts, but I could only think, *Will I survive this? Are my children at risk for breast cancer? What should I share and with whom?*

When I met with my oncologist the first week of November, I fully expected her to recommend six rounds of chemotherapy and maybe, just maybe, a few rounds of radiation. What I got was 16 rounds of chemotherapy, four every two weeks and then 12 EVERY week, likely followed by a minimum of 30 radiation treatments. I went numb. She threw in something about me being a perfect candidate for a study.

Trying to process all of this was just too much, and my best friend was dying. How could she help me to make reason out of this chaos? How could I possibly share this with her? I didn't, at least not initially. I waited a few days and tried to process it on my own.

First, being the good patient and morally conscious physician, I signed up for the research study.

Second, I followed all of my oncologist's recommandations. Third, I scheduled the dreaded rounds of chemo on Mondays, figuring I would then get on with my week. Nothing beat chemo for a reason to complain about starting a new work week.

When I told my mom of my treatment plans, I used phrases like "a few rounds" and "a few treatments." She had enough to worry about with helping the rest of our family cope and accept, as she had, the peace of her dying.

I was doing my best to cope, but my distressing condition was making it hard for me to keep things straight, which was further disheartening as clearly I was no longer the most organized person in the world. It was even hard to ask the right questions and easy to misunderstand the answers. I figured out a few things in the process:

> I brought someone with me to significant medical appointments. She supported me in whatever I needed her to do like ask additional questions, write down information, or be an actively listening fly on the wall.

> I asked as many questions as I had, repeatedly if necessarily. I didn't let anything, including my reputation as a doctor, stand in the way of understanding.

> I tried to keep an open mind to prevent myself from interpreting news as worse than it was.

> I shared the news.

There were a host of reasons why sharing about the big "C" was difficult, but I knew it would be more difficult to go it alone. I couldn't tell my number one confidant, but I needed someone to help me bear this. The more I thought about it, the more people I thought of who loved me, who would want to help, and who would even take offense if they didn't know. God forbid I let them down.

Then there was the other big "C"—chemotherapy. Chemotherapy makes the disease real, so much so that I wondered whether the benefits of treatment outweighed the side effects. I struggled with whether or not it was all worth it. Sadly, I could not always see the light at the end of the tunnel.

On November 19, 2008, the doctor placed a port-a-catheter in a vein in my upper chest, just below the collar bone. I began chemo on December 1st.

As a cancer patient my mind raced: *What side effects will I have? Will I suffer a lot from pain, fatigue, or nausea? Will I lose my hair?*

As a physician, I was already keenly aware of possible side effects and why the word chemotherapy was guaranteed to strike fear in the heart of any newly-diagnosed breast cancer patient. What I couldn't know was what was going to happen to *me* physically or emotionally.

I should have taken advantage of a support group where members had gone through it, could articulate my fears, and could remind me that the end of treatment was indeed in sight. They could have shifted my focus away from chemo as the bitter pill prescribed by the evil doctors who are in cahoots with big pharma to chemo being the best life-saving, science-based therapy that medicine had to offer. I needed support.

3

Inspiration through Tribulation

Sharing my story was cathartic. It even turned out to be inspiring for me and the select group of family members, close friends, and co-workers who I periodically updated via group email. (I didn't want to tell it over and over again.)

What I needed was for everyone to stop assuming that I was strong based on past experiences. I needed permission to be weak.

11-08-2008
Hi Everyone,
     My chemo will begin Dec. 1st. The first 4 treatments, consisting of 2 medications, will be every 2 weeks. Then I will receive one medication every week for 12 weeks and the study drug every 3 weeks for 12 weeks.

15

I'm looking forward to Thanksgiving. My youngest daughter pointed out to me last night that I needed to really enjoy the next couple of weeks as my birthday, Christmas, and New Year's will be during chemo, and I "probably won't have much fun." No joke!!

Continue to keep me in your prayers, and I thank you from the bottom of my heart.

Take care,

Me

Sheri,

I am sorry to hear that this is another rough day. I know you don't like to hear people constantly say, "You are going to be fine," because right now you are not fine. I'd probably be frustrated too because it may seem like people have no clue of what you're going through. Know that the words, while sometimes not quite what you want to hear, come from a good place. People, myself included, hate that we can't do more to get you through this. I hope it helps in some small way to know we care, love you, and if it was a matter of us willing and praying you to recovery, it would indeed already be done.

Please, take this one day, one week, one treatment at a time, while pushing yourself beyond where you think you can go. You've amazed yourself before with your capacity to endure, and you will need to call on that spirit and inner strength that God's blessed you with to get through this. Everything is going to be fine. I say it because I believe it.

Love you!

Lisa

After my third round of chemotherapy, my update went like this:

12-30-08
Hey Everyone,

Well, I had round 3 of chemo on the 29th (yesterday), and last night was horrible. The first 4 rounds are supposed to be the toughest, so you can imagine I'm counting down. This has by far been the worst experience of my life to date. The room felt like it was spinning, and I felt like my entire body was on fire.

This morning I feel a lot better. This patient role is not easy, and I'm thankful for the knowledge I have as a physician. Without it I might be too squeamish to take the truckload of medications they supply you to combat the side effects of the chemo.

My kids overheard me appreciating why some people choose not to go through chemo. They made me lock hands with them and promise that I would finish my treatment. I told them they were the reason I was going through this in the first place. There are certain accomplishments they will achieve that I MUST see.

Still blessed,
Sheri

These were two of the many precious responses I received:

Sheri,

I hesitated to respond, because I was seeking something supportive to say. I know and hate pain of any kind. I think people who are stoic and quietly endure pain are nuts. I think that you have the right view of these very rotten events.

May your children and God help you through this experience. Know that it will get better. The side effects will go away, but, in the meantime, do not go quietly into the night. Let the world know that you want those good times to return right now.

It is good to hear from you. It is the only way that we who care about you can share with you. Remember when it's bad that we are also with you. You are always in our prayers.

Al

Sheri,

I was at first sad to hear about your struggle with cancer, but the more I thought about it, the more I was convinced if anyone can stand up and fight it, it would be you.

I sat and chatted with your Dad the other week. It was amazing listening to him, how proud he was of what you have done and how much you have battled. He was so proud, but was he worried? No, he was adamant you had the character, the inner strength, and the faith to knock this out of the proverbial ball park. It was uplifting to see a father say such things. It was actually quite moving.

I only know a small part of your life and your beliefs, but you always leave such a huge impression on me when you are here. It is quite amazing. God has a plan with you, Sheri. He will give you the power to overcome this. He will. He's just that sort of guy.

God Bless

Paul

These warm notes did everything the kind writers intended them to do. They comforted and encouraged me. However, a huge dose of my determination to move forward with a will to live came from sitting with the weighty question—to treat or not to treat. It was time to put my knowledge from my education, training, and experience to use for me.

I sat and thought and prayed and listened, and here's what I realized: Cancer could do everything to me that chemotherapy could do (except make me lose my hair) and MUCH MORE. I had seen more patients than I cared to admit fight and suffer and die from cancer, but to die from untreated cancer would be sicker than the worst horror movie:

- Dying from untreated cancer could mean suffering with unrelenting pain that would leave me with the choice of lingering drugged up with narcotics or dying in agony.

- Dying from untreated cancer could mean unrelenting vomiting from a bowel obstruction.

- Dying from untreated cancer could mean using a nasogastric tube or a tube sticking out of my stomach to drain my digestive juices to prevent me from throwing up.

- Dying from untreated cancer could mean bleeding in many forms, even into the brain, because I didn't have enough platelets to clot.

- Dying from untreated cancer could mean dramatic weight loss and muscle atrophy. (I imagined myself looking like a Nazi concentration camp survivor, starving African, or famine victim with cheeks so sunken my face looked like the skull underlying it.)

∽ Dying from untreated cancer could mean my lungs progressively filling with fluid from tumor infiltration. (I imagined choking on my own secretions, having progressive shortness of breath, and feeling an unrelenting suffocation with no possibility of relief ever.)

∽ Dying from untreated cancer could mean having my belly filled with ascites fluid due to my liver being chock full of tumor.

∽ Dying from cancer could mean a progressive decline in my mental function due to brain metastases.

∽ Other non-chemo medical options could alleviate the symptoms associated with terminal cancer, but all too often they could not reverse the disease process. Even with those options, relief would require me to accept treatment.

∽ Finally, the very best hospice could minimize symptoms for significant periods of time, but there would be nothing "healthy" or pleasant about dying from cancer. Dying in the comfort of hospice would still mean losing control, becoming too weak to get up by myself, to feed myself, to go to the bathroom by myself, to bathe myself, or to do anything other than lay in my bed and wait for the end.

Although chemotherapy had already proven to be almost as dreadful as it could possibly be in my case, I considered it quite viable and didn't question it again after considering this clear distinction. I knew that I treasured life and living much more than any body part, so surgery and scars and chemotherapy's side effects and radiation would be my choice as long as I could hope to live. After all, when I detected the lump early with that type of cancer in it, I had given myself a 75 percent chance of more than a five-year survival.

Feeling strength from these revelations, I womaned up, took my chemo, and took my place in the 75 percent! When I refused to give up, the greatest tragedy of my life turned out to be one of the greatest blessings.

Then in the quiet, closing moments of my meditation, I reached a most important caveat to my decision: Death was inevitable for me no matter my choice. It is inevitable for every person on Earth. I would, therefore, fully support the choices of others, especially those who might choose to soar with me in their desires to treat or to accept comfort, to live or to die.

April 20, 2009
Hey Everyone,

I know it's been awhile since I emailed because multiple complications had me depressed. Today, I have good news to tell. Today was my last of 15 chemo treatments!!!

There were so many times that I asked God why, but every time I went immediately into thanking Him, knowing things could be so much worse.

You all have prayed, encouraged, and supported me in ways that have kept me smiling and
away from the breaking point.
Many thanks and much love to all!!!
Sheri

Sheri,

Even though I am very saddened to hear of your constant pain and discomfort, I am amazed at the strength you
have in light of your problems. You are a shining light to
everyone you touch. I guess God has His way to teach and
show all of us how strong we can be and how much we can
tolerate. Your faith is refreshing and pure. I know you will
get through this. You are leading the line for everyone by
your words and actions.

Continue to battle on, my dear. You can beat this, as
you have shown so far. Don't give in.

You will be in my daily prayers,
Paul

All the emotions that I was experiencing were
completely normal, but I was hard on myself. Sometimes well meaning, sometimes insensitive off-color
comments from people who don't know "the right
thing to say" also added to my gloom.

A dear friend of mine, who is a young survivor
of testicular cancer and an awesome writer and film-
maker, shared his thoughts on *Huffington Post* enti-
tled, "Don't Say This to a Cancer Patient." His words
reverberated with the thoughts of every cancer survivor I knew. He said this to friends and loved ones of
cancer patients or caregivers:

For starters, we know that you love us, care

for us, and want to comfort us, and we love and adore you for it, and are extremely grateful for your compassion and kindness. With that said, we will internally, and sometimes externally, tear you a new anus for saying any of the following platitudes:

1. "This may be hard to hear, but..."
2. "I can relate."
3. "This is part of God's bigger plan."
4. "God doesn't give you a cross you can't bear."

Most people didn't feel comfortable with silence. They needed to say "something." Depending on the day, I might have educated them that "nothing" was much better than "something."

My dear friend Dan so wisely admonished me not to get mad when I heard the words, "I'm sorry you're going through this." If there were one sure thing a close friend or family member could say to make me feel even a shred of a whiff of a modicum of better, it would be, "I will be here for you in any way you need, in any way I can." After that it was up to me to direct them in how I needed help. Otherwise, they'd help in whatever way they could figure out, which might not be what I needed. Maybe I needed for someone to come to my house every day to check on me; maybe I needed them to back off, except when I called on them. I figured out not to expect people to guess.

What I needed was for everyone to stop assuming that I was strong based on past experiences. I needed permission to be weak. Over and over people said,

"You're strong. You're going to get through this."
"Only 12 more chemo treatments. It'll be over before
you know it." Or my favorite, "You never looked like
you had a sick day in your life!"

Despite the occasional crazy comments, I had
wonderful social support from friends and family.
We learned together.

When people offered, "What can I do to help?" at
first I would turn it down.

"Oh, nothing right now. We're just fine," I'd say.
Sometimes I wanted privacy; sometimes I resisted bur-
dening anyone.

Later, I learned to respond with completely honest, specific answers, believing the people who really
did want to help me and matching my need with their
offer. It's not like I didn't need help with a ride to
the doctor, housecleaning, meals, yard work, or child
care. When I needed extra help, I asked.

I learned also that some of them needed my
companionship as much as I needed theirs. Often-
times, helping me resolved their frustrating feeling of
helplessness.

4

Churchy Chatter

"Where is your faith?" was a question I heard not infrequently once I settled on treatment. Some church members thought I was not "releasing faith" by "having all that treatment." Criticizing my faith was akin to criticizing my intellect or my cute face or any other important part of me, so that question would put me on the defensive if I wasn't careful. However, my faith did take a turn and a few leaps during this distressing health challenge.

I had grown up in a church where the members believed in faith healing. Faith healing is healing through spiritual means. Believers assert that religious faith, prayer, and/or other rituals can bring about healing. According to adherents, faith can stimulate a

Now that I was free of other people's religion and had stabilized myself in thankfulness, I could make a new assessment of my spiritual life.

divine presence and power able to correct disease and disability.

For some of my friends and family, it was all or none. Going through "all that treatment" made me an infidel, almost. I obviously didn't have faith that God could heal me. Zealots told story after story of how some person was sick but prayed, and God healed him. It didn't seem to matter that the person merely had a common headache! Their retort was, "Well he could have had cancer, too, but God healed him."

Well, I wouldn't stoop so low as to criticize someone's faith ... but if I would, I would ask why they couldn't believe that God would bless my treatment to work? Why wouldn't He ultimately be the One to heal me?

Faith turn: I finally decided that all of those other people were not me. (Whew!) Their religion could be a source of strength for them, but I was not a fan of the word "religion" when used in their sense. My source of strength came from my spirituality, my relationship with God. I decided to take a spiritual road to confronting my problems. This made all the difference in this sensitive season of my life.

My problem was that I needed healing, but I didn't seem to be making any headway toward receiving it even though I already knew the principles of receiving healing in theory. What I had never quite grasped, however, was that I could just *rest* in Jesus' finished work of healing for me. When I read Joseph Prince's books, *Destined to Reign* and *Unmerited Favor*, I learned a whole lot more about grace and the finished work of Jesus than I'd ever known previously.

I also learned to be *thankful* that my healing was a done deal—even if the symptoms persisted for a while and even if I had to complete all recommended treatment. That thankfulness did something to my inner person. I began to feel supernatural faith arise inside for whatever healing I needed. In fact, as I persisted in thanking God that Jesus had already done it for me, I found myself really settling down deep into that faith. I really believed I *was* healed, and that in the end I would be healed.

As I thanked God, my heart became joyful—and peaceful, too. I found that my thoughts were focusing on Jesus instead of health issues. I was coming into the abiding place that Jesus talked about in John 15:7, *"If you abide in me, and my words abide in you, you shall ask what you will, and it shall be done for you." (King James Version)*

The best part of all was that thanking the Lord led me into a deeper love for Him. As I thanked Him from my heart, His presence gathered around me.

I began using thankfulness often, as often as circumstances appeared overwhelming. I practiced it when prayer felt like it wasn't working. I'd begin thanking the Lord aloud! I'd thank Him for hearing me and for pouring out the answer. I'd get real happy in a hurry. Anxiety just couldn't hang around, neither could the temptation to doubt. Faith and joy would bubble up inside.

Both as a physician and as a patient, I have watched

spiritual questions and answers emerge as people tried to make sense of their illnesses and their lives. That would often be true for their loved ones, too. Whether they found new faith or newfound strength from existing faith (my case) or, less commonly, no faith at all, enduring the ordeal was always personal.

In my experience, I found the following to be true:

- A spiritual counselor helped me find comforting answers to hard questions.

- Spiritual practices, such as forgiveness or confession, were reassuring and brought me a sense of peace.

- My search for the meaning of suffering led to spiritual answers that comforted me.

- Spiritual support from a community of people who were there to help provided priceless strength to me and my family members.

Now that I was free of other people's religion and had stabilized myself in thankfulness, I could make a new assessment of my spiritual life. That was a refreshing, grown-up exercise. Lots of eye opening moments ensued, the first of which was directly relevant to how I was perceiving God in the context of my health challenge.

I perceived faith as a positive notion, akin to trust in God. Active faith, then, would aim to remove negative thoughts about the illness, which could easily dominate me, and replace them with trust in God using a positive attitude. I chose this approach intentionally and followed it with the same discipline I had used in every other area of my life. Eventually, I felt confident that everything would be fine. I credited that confidence with the fact that I energized myself spiritually. I came to believe that I would be able to accept whatever the outcome was to be. I knew that I could do everything in this life that I was meant to do through Christ who strengthened me (Philippians 4:13).

When I made that statement prior to my battle with breast cancer, I was affirming my desire for God to provide favorable outcomes to my endeavors. My thinking went something like this: *I can do anything I set my mind to if I simply believe,* i.e., *I can achieve any personal goal by faith. Get this job. Win this game. Ace this test.*

Through the cancer ordeal I learned that the affirmation had little or nothing to do with my personal achievements in the face of severe odds; it was not about my achievements at all. My use of that Bible verse changed significantly to underscore my desire to be content in every circumstance, even when things seemed to be at their worst.

Byron Yawn, the senior pastor of Community Bible Church in Nashville, Tennessee, spoke about the affirmation this way: "I can fail to achieve my goals and still trust my Savior's love. Or, I can have cancer. Or, I can lose everything. Or, I can be fired. I can "do all this" because of who Jesus is."

I thought about the potential danger of wrongly thinking that I could do anything I set my mind to, especially in situations that were not guaranteed to turn out favorably—say, an aggressive form of breast cancer. What if I couldn't "do" it? What if things didn't work out—no matter how much I believed? My failure might have called into question the goodness of God. I have seen that kind of thinking rob countless hurting and weak people of the truth. As strange as it may sound, there is power in weakness.

My weak, cancer-challenged refrain sounded something like, "Lord, why won't you help me?" How often I had moaned those words. I viewed God's hand as closed with His help tucked away inside. I thought I just had to do the right things, and then He'd open His hand to help me.

There were times when the good girl/do gooder in me couldn't figure out what those "right things" were. I often felt ashamed of that. Then there were other times when I felt God's help flooding my life. I had to figure out the key.

What I learned was that when I was connected to God's help, three things were in order: 1) I was committed to doing it God's way. 2) I was willing to wait on Him. 3) I was devoted to God's will.

God's Way

When I took a good hard stare at that shame I felt when I didn't get it right, I had to be honest about the motivation behind my prayers. Asking, "God, why won't you help?" was insisting that God help me my way. When I remembered that God's ways were above my ways, my perspective changed (Isaiah 55:9). I stopped expecting God to help in ways I prescribed, and I began to lose that "God isn't helping me" feeling. I began praying, "God, will you help me to recognize your help?" It worked.

The good news was that I had chosen and received the God of my faith carefully. His hand had always been open to help me. When it seemed that His help was unavailable, the problem wasn't His closed hand, but rather my closed heart. I tended to refuse God's help the same way a rebellious teen would refuse parental assistance, because she thought she knew better. God would help, but I would refuse the kind of help He was offering me.

When I insisted that God help me my way, that was pride, pure and simple. When I sought God's help in humility, I was acknowledging that ultimately He knew best. Then I could relax. That was liberating in the context of a health challenge over which I had no control.

God's Timing

Impatience sabotaged my faith and my ability to recognize and receive God's help. If God didn't deliver a truckload of help at lightning speed, my feeble mind—fueled by self-pity—immediately assumed that God didn't want to help me ... because I was unworthy. (Back to the shame.) I would then quickly begin to look for help elsewhere. After a while my prayers were not pregnant with expectation or faith or heart or intimacy. Sometimes my prayers were merely words.

I took a good hard look at the pattern of my behavior and saw a completely logical root. I found myself wondering, *If Scripture promises that God is an ever-present help I can trust when I face trouble (Psalm 33:20; 46:1; Isaiah 40:31), then why do I have to wait for His help?* I came to realize that God gives enough help for the moment, and that I may need to wait for the next installment. God didn't just want to give me His help, His stuff; He wanted to give me Himself so that my relationship with Him could grow. The more I figured this out, the more I have found Him to be totally worth the wait.

God's Will

The last question that framed out my refreshed faith challenged me to the core. As a professed follower of God, was I dedicated to God's will? Was I open to what God wanted? Did I trust Him with me? Sometimes not.

For example, I have participated in various organizations based on my impression that God wanted me to make a contribution there. When things have gotten rough, however, I have prayed for Him to get me out of there. My idea of help was God finding someone to replace me! In those instances I sensed no help from God, because I was asking for help to go against God's will instead of noticing the help He was offering me in the situation. All too often, I have wanted a way out, rather than help from God to make it through.

Grappling with God's will in the face of a life-threatening illness was complicated. I had what I would call a natural pull to live, but a charge to accept life or death in peaceful faith. I viewed God as the giver of all life, but that life spectrum spanned Earth to Heaven, from the here and now to the life that continues after death. Would I remain dedicated to God's will if He wanted me to go to the next life? With children and friends and dreams, etc., leaving here would be a major move.

When I would pray, "If it's your will for me to continue, I will; not my will but yours be done," then I would receive God's strength, comfort, and grace to complete my assignment. Staying dedicated to God's will—even in difficult times—helped me to see God's purposes, which were so much more noble and far-reaching than mine. I have learned over time that God helps those who are dedicated to His will.

In my faith evolution, it was the unpredictable swings of life (want, prosperity, health) that I was learning to traverse by focusing on the higher power that governed my life. I accepted that my faith was not about my dreams, my goals, my agenda, and getting God to assist me with them. It was about me doing God's will, working out God's salvation plan, even when it involved suffering, loss, and the unexpected.

No longer would I take good health and well-being

for granted. Even while I was well and it was easy to forget that the ability to talk, for example, is a gift, I would count my blessings. I wouldn't wait for a serious illness to notice. It would be part of my daily prayers. In this way serious illness brought me closer to God. It was either that or make me angry and resolved to never pray again.

This decision reminded me of a good story in the second book of Kings in the Bible. It would be relevant for those who are Christians or not, avid church-goers or occasional Christmas visitors. This was the story of Naaman, a great general in the army who had contracted leprosy. He immersed himself in the Jordan River as instructed by the prophet Elisha. When he came out of the water he was cured of leprosy, and from that point he no longer doubted God's mercy.

Like Naaman, I received an opportunity to discover God through a life-threatening health challenge. The way I faced the challenge determined whether I would grow spiritually or die to God. It took quite a journey to settle into that level of faith and assurance.

5

Be Still My Heart

The sun never shined on chemo Mondays. It was always clouded over by the all-consuming question, "Will my hair fall out?" I had decided to braid my hair in cornrows (French braids) about a week prior to my first chemotherapy session and wear short wigs just in case.

My mom's medication regimen hadn't affected her lovely mane at all. The only change was the length, because she couldn't comb to the middle of her back anymore. Sometimes *I didn't want to live without my mom, but I didn't care in that moment that my girls would have to live without theirs.* I'd find her lying in bed rolling her hair because, "You never know who may stop by."

Her medications did take their toll on her voice though, giving it that drug-induced lull. That frightened me. I was afraid that she really was leaving me. I was also angry that things weren't going as I planned.

By then we were supposed to be spending her last days cuddled up together, looking forward to Heaven, but I could not even visit her on Mondays! When I did, she would spend the day vomiting, and I would have difficulty breathing. It's a phenomenon called transference where patients switch symptoms.

By Wednesday I could see her, but my white blood cell count was so low that too much movement would send me hurling. Hearing my voice also made her sicker. So, we didn't snuggle. She lay in the bed, I sat quietly in the chair, and we held hands. Sometimes we had the energy to look at each other.

On one such occasion, she woke up briefly to shift positions. We locked eyes and I whispered, "I love you." She returned to her sleep oblivion, and my heart broke. *She didn't hear me. She didn't understand what I said*. Before I could shed a tear, she said, "I love you, too!"

That was it. I broke all the rules. Before I knew what I was doing, I was sprawled across her chest and sobbing uncontrollably. *How did I get here? Why was all of this happening?* I buried my head in my mother's arms, and her hands cradled my neck.

The comfort I drew from that embrace was beyond words. I quickly pulled it together and got back on the plan, but I still yearn for her touch.

My final round of "the really bad chemo" (Adriamycin and Cytoxan) was scheduled for Monday, January

13, 2009, and then I would start the comparatively smooth sailing chemo (Taxol) weekly for 12 weeks. Things were looking up. Then again, depending on how I was randomized in the clinical drug research trial, I could end up receiving chemo weekly for one full year.

By the Saturday before treatment, I should have been sufficiently recovered from the previous treatment. I should have been able to enjoy the weekend somewhat, but I felt rundown all day. I couldn't seem to shake the malaise.

Suddenly, I had a crushing chest pain, which meant one of two things: a heart attack or a blood clot in my lungs. It was the girls' weekend with their dad, so no one else was home. I should have called 911, but doctors can be the worst patients. Instead, I placed my life insurance policy in plain view, prayed for God to forgive my sins, comfort and keep my girls, and let my mom's transition be smooth, and went to bed. I didn't want to live without my mom, but I didn't care in that moment that my girls would have to live without theirs. Suffering had made me selfish, self-centered, and single-minded.

I drifted off to sleep fully expecting to awake in Paradise, pain free, cancer free, and free. Instead, I woke up in pain, with cancer, and bound by the impending loss of my mom. I was pissed and depressed that I was still alive.

I got dressed for my 10-year-old daily workout, which had kept me sane through chemo, but I couldn't do it. The girls came home to see me lying on the couch and shouted, "What's wrong!"

"You look green!" their dad told me. "Why didn't you get help?"

Easy for you to say. You have no idea what I'm going through, I thought, inconsiderate of his impending solo fatherhood. *You don't have cancer, and your mother isn't dying. You can handle it!*

He convinced me to call my oncologist who of course said, "Go to the emergency room NOW!" Not wanting to be accused of being a bad patient, which had already been established when I didn't call 911, I heeded her advice.

Because my chief complaint was chest pain, they took me back for evaluation immediately. Testing showed it wasn't a blood clot. *Good, I can go home.* It couldn't be a heart attack, because I was the healthiest person I knew. However, my cardiac enzymes came back slightly elevated. To my dismay, they admitted me to the telemetry unit for constant cardiac monitoring.

My primary concern was not my heart, but how this ER fiasco was jeopardizing my final chemo round the next morning. Heaven forbid that this cardiac work up delay it! I called my oncologist and told her to send the chemo to the 7th floor.

"We'll have to transfer you to the third floor, because we don't have clearance for chemo on telemetry," she replied.

Meanwhile, the cardiologist sent me down for a CT angiogram to get a better look at my heart. When I returned, my oncologist reported that the cardiologist was concerned about my ability to withstand the chemo treatment with everything else that was going on. *What "everything else?!"*

I burst into tears. I was finally coming to grips with my cancer diagnosis, but now my head was swimming with complications. I began to question what I did to deserve this punishment. Then I wondered, *Is there a purpose for this nightmare?*

My cardiologist gave me the news: 70% stenosis of my right coronary artery. It wasn't blocked by a cholesterol plaque; it was squished by my pulmonary artery and my aorta. Apparently, I'd had this condition since birth, but the chemo was causing spasms. The cardiologist scheduled me for an early morning coronary angioplasty to place a stent in my artery so that I wouldn't have a full blown heart attack.

A cardiac catheterization, also known as an angiogram, is a diagnostic procedure for evaluating blood flow to the heart. It enables physicians to view two-dimensional, live-action X-rays of a patient's heart and the surrounding coronary arteries. Digital imaging, in which a computer translates the X-ray images, helps cardiologists determine if the blood vessels, valves, and chambers are functioning properly. Most cardiac catheterizations are same day, outpatient procedures. The patient is awake but sedated. A thin tube, called a catheter, is threaded through the patient's groin into the artery leading to his or her heart. A contrast dye in the catheter illuminates the heart and its vessels on an X-ray monitor. After the test is completed, the catheter is removed. At most medical centers, interventional or treatment procedures to open blocked arteries are performed after the diagnostic part of the cardiac catheterization is complete. For certain people, heart disease treatment can be achieved without surgery.

A cardiac catheterization is generally safe, but there are risks with any invasive procedure. Special precautions are taken to decrease these risks, which can include the following:

- Bleeding around the point of puncture
- Abnormal heart rhythms
- Blood clots
- Infection
- Allergic reaction to the dye
- Stroke
- Heart attack
- Perforation of a blood vessel
- Air embolism (introduction of air into a blood vessel, which can be life-threatening)
- Death

Angioplasty is a non-surgical procedure that can be used if an angiogram shows blocked heart arteries. The doctor will move the catheter into the artery that has blockage, open the artery, and clear the blockage.

Stents are commonly placed during interventional procedures such as angioplasties to help keep the coronary artery open. A stent is a small metal mesh tube that acts as a scaffold to provide support inside your coronary artery. Some stents contain medicine and are designed to reduce the risk of re-blockage (restenosis). A balloon catheter, placed over a guide wire, is used to insert the stent into the narrowed coronary artery. Once in place, the balloon tip is inflated and the stent expands to the size of the artery, holding it open. The balloon is then deflated and removed while the stent stays in place permanently. Over several weeks, the artery heals around the stent.

In our pre-surgery talk, the cardiologist told me that had I gotten on that treadmill, I could have died. I didn't really know how to feel about hearing that, because being dead was what I wanted, I thought.

Then he infuriated me when he went into the whole possible side effects discussion. I asked him, "Do we really have to do this? Every time I hear the infamous 'This occurs in less than 1% of the population,' I end up in that 1%!"

He gave me a sleep aid, because it was obvious I was a little stressed. It didn't work. I tossed and turned all night.

The sun barreled into my room along with the nurse and technicians who would take me down for surgery. I reminded my cardiologist that I wanted to be awake throughout the procedure, because I wanted to see the artery that was causing all of this trouble.

Lying on the operating room table, looking up at all of the bright lights and feeling the chill in the air, I felt alone. I expected to feel warm and relaxed after getting my "twilight" relaxation drugs, but I felt cold and scared. The doc numbed my right groin area and started the procedure.

After two and a half hours and two trays of catheters and stents, none of them fit properly! For two and a half hours I lay there looking at the TV monitor, watching my torturous artery subvert every strategic measure my highly educated and well-equipped cardiologist attempted.

Looking dejected, he admitted, "Nothing fits. I'm sorry, but I must stop."

"You did what you could. Just let me be," I replied.

The following day my cardiologist released me with a lifelong treatment plan of blood thinners and Lipitor to stave off blockage and my premature demise. It was time to send an update.

01-16-09

Hi Everyone,

I was discharged yesterday with reduced heart pumping power and reduced coronary artery blood flow (from a birth defect I didn't know I had). They couldn't do a stent placement, so they may have to consider bypass surgery or continue with the 4 medications I've started. I will not be receiving the 4th round of Adriamycin and Cytoxan and they are removing me from the clinical trial. I will start phase 2 of my chemo with Taxol (which is not supposed to affect the heart) on Monday, Jan. 19th.

I'm baffled and overwhelmed as to why this is all happening, but grateful that it was discovered and that I didn't have a massive heart attack during a workout. I've cried more in the past three days than I have since discovering my breast cancer. I believe I once said that the cancer and chemo had been my worst experience to date. Well, they WERE.

I've discovered that my time to LIVE is NOW. The little things I took for granted--having an appetite, eating when I wanted, breathing normally, having the energy to do just about anything that needed to be done—are no longer little, and I no longer take them for granted.

Please take my advice: DO NOT SWEAT THE SMALL STUFF, LIVE TODAY, AND MAKE SURE YOUR LOVED ONES KNOW THEY ARE LOVED.

Continue to keep me in your thoughts and prayers. I will continue to fight the good fight, because the race isn't given to the swift, neither to the strong, but to the one who endures until the end!!

Love to you all,
Sheri

Here are just a couple of the endearing responses I received:

Dear Sheri,

You are one in a million, medically, professionally, but MOST of all spiritually and emotionally!! You are awesome and ever so right. I have maintained for the last 23 years of my life that the only true gift we have is our health. All the money and possessions in the world mean nothing without our health. NOW comes this new enlightenment of the importance of faith, not that I didn't know it. I just don't think I appreciated it until you came into my life. So many talk the talk, but I've watched and listened to you walk the talk. You are AWESOME!!! and loved and prayed for and thought of so often fondly as are your girls. I pray that they find the strength and faith their Mom has.

Did I tell you, you are AWESOME?!!!

Love ya! Stay warm!

Karen

Sheri,

All these letters made me really understand what a strong person you are. There is so much we all can learn from you in our lives, which we take for granted. The last time I met you in Barrington, you left me with the thought, "She's such a nice and friendly person." I remember you were eating a lunch bag of fruits. You looked so healthy. I just can't believe this is happening to you.

I think I have prayed for you more than I have prayed for my mom or anybody else in my life. I want God to give your health back, not just for your daughters, but for all of us praying for you.

Thank you for considering us as your family to update us about your health. I didn't want to bother you writing or calling, but my eyes couldn't stop tearing, so I decided to write to you.

I and my family prayers are always with you,
Indu

I was initially happy to skip the last bad chemo round. Then, I panicked, *What if I didn't get enough and the cancer comes back?* For weeks I had to shake those thoughts. I tried to encourage myself several times a day. *It is what it is.* Plus, the bad chemo was the culprit that would take out my hair; the Taxol would only inhibit the re-growth.

On the day after my attempted angioplasty, I decided to take out my braids. I'd see if any of my crowning glory remained. My right groin throbbed in pain, and my scalp had never been so sensitive. My younger daughter, Kiana, held my hand; my older daughter, Kirsten, began to take down my braids. The whole process was excruciating, and it was taking an eternity to finish. Out of curiosity about how many more braids she had to take down, I decided to take a feel for myself. Well, I could have heated my head and used it for a hot stone massage. My fingers slid around in search of at least a single strand of hair. I was bald. Apparently, Kirsten wasn't taking down my braids; she was taking them off. My hair came out with every stroke of the comb. Within fifteen minutes, I lost 100,000 hairs.

In my efforts to endure the pain, I hadn't noticed the heavy breathing coming from Kirsten as she practiced extreme self-control to hold back the gut-wrenching sobs that wanted to erupt. I also hadn't noticed the stream of tears raining down Kiana's face.

I needed a minute. I wanted to run to the bathroom and assess the damage, but the wound in my right groin still throbbed and oozed blood. I walked gingerly. When I finally looked into the mirror, a complete stranger stared back at me. She was bald, thin but puffy from steroids, pale, and frail. Her eyes looked distant and lost. She was sad, depressed, despondent, lonely, mad, and UGLY. I didn't know this woman and I didn't want to know her. She was both empty and complicated. I wanted her to go away. Tears streamed down this foreigner's face. I looked around for something to break the mirror.

My daughters joined me on either side, and Kirsten said, "Mommy, it's OK. Now put your bandana on and don't look at it anymore." I did as I was told. Sleep did not come easily for me that night.

6
Glory Bound

Mom and I grew weaker every week. She would say, "I'm ready to see Jesus. If He is not going to heal me, then I'm ready to go home."

A stern rebuke always followed: "As long as there is life there is hope," or "Girl, you look good! Some people well don't look as good as you do sick," and, of course, "Where is your faith?" They were looking at it all wrong.

Mom had lived a full life, and God had given her peace about going home. It was so unfair and unkind for people to forbid her from experiencing it.

I was the only one who would allow her to express her happiness with each step of planning her home-going. Only I, understandably, would work on it with her. It was depressing, but she *needed* to do it.

Crossing the threshold of their bedroom felt like a dream, her small frame lacking her effervescence, promise, and life.

Getting through her list of "Things to Do" kept her alive and gave her purpose. Diligently making arrangements for a true celebration made her giddy at times. Picking the colors, her casket (which would be closed), the casket floral cascade, flowers, and photos for her collage excited her. We also organized how her printed program would look.

She was thrilled that one day she and my dad would have a combined headstone proudly displaying "Wife" and "Husband" over them. She told my dad not to spend the rest of his life alone. One day she even announced, "I wish I wasn't confined to this bed. I would take you out and find your next wife." However, it wasn't until he visited the gravesite for the first time and saw their names and titles that he realized something. Mom may have been fine with him having a temporary wife, but she wasn't going to be buried next to my dad! He laughed, saying, "Oh, your mom … she was a tricky little something!"

She would always say she was "planning to live but preparing to die," until the time came when we were simply preparing. This exercise was supposed to spare the family the agony of having to do so after she was gone. I helped her on whatever project she wanted to tackle, smiled when she smiled, went home, went to my closet, and cried myself dry.

My mom showed me how to die with dignity and grace. She suffered silently for the greater part of 13 years until silence became impossible. She fought long and hard, but in the end she tired and made peace with her legacy.

As I would sit watching her sleep, I'd noticed how small and frail she looked in that enormous hospital bed in that huge bedroom with all that clutter. I used to think her room was nicely appointed, but something had changed in me. Not a drop of the stuff in that living tomb could bring her comfort: king-sized bed, armoire, chest of drawers, night stands, jewelry chest, or entertainment center. It was then that material possessions began to lose their value to me.

Nothing in that room could help her pass the time. Nothing made her breathing any less labored. Not even me—her youngest baby, the executor of her estate, the college graduate, the doctor. I couldn't extend her life, couldn't take a breath for her, couldn't die for her.

I found myself counting. It took 28–30 breaths per minute to keep my mom alive. Her rhythmic breaths took me out of myself until she sprung out of her sleepy stupor.

"Hi," she said.

"Hi," I replied.

"How long have you been here?"

"A little over an hour."

"Oh."

"Do you notice something?"

Mom shrugged her shoulders.

"I'm wearing one of your wigs."

"Oh, yeah."

I pulled the wig off to reveal my smooth globe where beautiful, shoulder-length, medium brown hair used to lay. My mom looked at me sheepishly and pulled the covers over her eyes. She looked like a little girl who wanted to laugh but, instead, covered her impish smile to help me save face. She looked so adorable. I pulled back the covers to reveal the cutest smirk, teaching me, again, it didn't matter. India Arie's song "I Am Not My Hair" then rang very true to me.

Hair loss and nasty chemo aside, I expected my body to tolerate the Taxol. To my dismay, it did not. I developed symptoms of nerve damage (neuropathy) and my white blood cell count remained dangerously low. I continued the visits, but they became more difficult, both physically and emotionally.

I'm not sure if I felt so near death because of her or me. Every message we shared seemed so final:

"I've loved and will always love you like no other."

"Although I'll miss you, I'll carry you in my heart always."

"You've given me just what I needed."

It was funny how just three years prior, I was prepared for her to leave and to be delivered from her pain. Now, I was NOT ready. It seemed incomprehensible that I would be fighting the greatest battle of my life and losing my best friend at the same time. How could this all be a part of God's great plan for my life? Still, life went on.

I woke up on February 16, 2009 feeling very much out of sorts. Everything I did took major effort. My arm felt like lead when I brushed my teeth, I was out of breath after washing my face, and showering just about annihilated me!

I very gingerly dressed myself and slipped on my

short and sassy "off to chemo" hair to frame my paler than usual face. I expected to see "Welcome to Timbuktu" when I pulled up to the hospital, because that's how long it felt like I had driven. When I walked into the oncologist's office, all eyes were on me. Apparently, I looked like the walking dead. The nurse quickly checked my white blood cell count and discovered it was below 1.8. Below 2.0 there would be no chemo.

I felt betrayed. My body betrayed me. The medical guidelines betrayed me. Christians who weren't praying hard enough betrayed me!

They shot me with Neulasta to help my body produce more white blood cells and told me they'd try again the next day. After expending a lifetime of energy getting dressed to go to the hospital to get toxic drugs injected into me that would hopefully prevent the potentially life-threatening cancer from eating me alive, all I heard was, "Sorry, not today!" Here was another delay in getting this whole chemo ordeal over and done with. Not surprisingly, within hours of the injection I experienced dizziness, nosebleeds, shortness of breath, pain in my arms and legs, and bone pain.

Serious Neulasta side effects may include
- sudden or severe pain in left upper stomach spreading to the shoulder;
- severe dizziness, skin rash, or flushing (warmth, redness, or tingly feeling);
- rapid breathing or feeling short of breath;
- signs of infection such as fever, chills, sore throat, flu symptoms, easy bruising or bleeding (nosebleeds,

bleeding gums), loss of appetite, nausea and vomiting, mouth sores, unusual weakness; or

∞ bruising, swelling, pain, redness, or a hard lump where the injection was given.

Less serious Neulasta side effects may include
∞ bone pain;

∞ arms or legs pain; or

∞ bruising, swelling, pain, redness, or a hard lump at the injection site.

While lying in bed, praying that the shot would work so that I could resume my toxin-taking schedule the following morning, an overwhelming sadness overtook me. I called my dad and asked how my mom was doing. He said she'd been sleeping all day. I called the hospice nurse for more details.

Mom's blood pressure was 70/40, and she was breathing at nearly 32 times per minute at rest on nearly 12 liters of oxygen. The nurse didn't expect that she would make it through the night. I knew she wouldn't.

I had promised my mom that I would be there when she transitioned from this life to the next, and nothing, not even a white blood cell count so low you can't get chemo, would prevent me from being by her side.

I called my grandmother to give her the status. She appeared unbelieving.

I told my daughters that their Grammy was going to die that night. Kirsten asked if I needed her to go with me.

"No baby. Mommy will be fine. Just pray for my strength," I replied.

Kiana said, "I can't go Ma. I want to remember her the way she was when I last saw her." I totally understood.

A huge part of me wanted to hide in those wonderful, safe memories, too. I was not looking forward to how her final moments would make her look, sound, or smell.

To say the ride over was somber would be a drastic understatement. I could hear my grandmother, aunt, and cousin trying to make small talk. I sat in the back struggling for every breath, especially through my respiratory mask that was protecting me from all of their normal but deadly germs.

Forty minutes later we pulled up to the gated retirement community that my parents had called home for 12 years. I wrestled with the finality of the moment until I got out of the car. My sense of foreboding left. Strength and power that can only be described as supernatural came over me.

My parents' bedroom was immediately to the left upon entering their house. The moment my dad opened the door, the scent of death permeated my nostrils. Crossing the threshold of their bedroom felt like a dream, her small frame lacking her effervescence, promise, and life.

Just a few days prior, these same family members had visited my mom, and, although she was very weak and slept most of the time, she had still tried to engage us and answer our feeble little questions. Between naps, we would smile at each other. Once she awak-ened and looked around the room, she locked eyes momentarily with her mother, sister, and nephew. When she caught my eyes, she simply said, "They have to let me go!"

Suddenly my grandmother appeared very preoc-cupied with wanting to know if my mom recognized everyone in the room. So every time my mom would wake up, my grandmother would ask, "Do you know who I am?" "What about this woman over here?" pointing to my aunt. She asked those questions like a mother would ask her 2-year-old at a small family gathering.

At times my mom would stare for a very long time before she replied, but she always got it right. When my grandmother finally asked, "Who is this?" point-ing at me, my mom immediately answered, "That's MY baby."

This night was different. The woman we had seen a few days before could have run a marathon com-pared to the woman lying in that hospital bed.

It was 8:28 pm, and my mom was hooked up to two oxygen concentrators that were rigged to try to deliver an unprecedented 12 liters of oxygen. Her breathing was no longer 32 beats per minute, but rather a specialized breathing called Cheyne-Stokes.

Cheyne-Stokes respirations are a pattern of irregular breathing often seen in the last days of life. Breathing can be very deep and rapid, followed by periods of slow shallow breaths, or episodes of apnea, where an individual stops breathing altogether for a period of time. Cheyne-Stokes respirations are common during the dying process from any illness.

Having been at the bedside of hundreds of dying people during my career, I recognized death when I walking through the front door, even before I laid eyes on her. I slipped into doctor-mode and headed to the right side, the examination side, of her bed. I knew she wasn't my patient, but I wanted to check her vitals and evaluate her status. It was the end.

I slipped back into daughter-mode and held her hand, caressed her face, and ran my fingers through her hair. I told her that I loved her, and I reminded her that I had asked God to let me be with her when she transitioned. He had answered my prayer.

My dad became restless. He started emptying out the garbage and moving things to no place in particular.

"Daddy, you need to come and say goodbye to your wife," I said in a voice that didn't sound like mine.

He stopped his incessant pacing, ran to her side, and said, "I love you. I will always love you. You gave me the best years of my life, and I'm going to miss you."

Her breathing became slower and more shallow with more frequent episodes of apnea. My family noticed it as well. I asked if anyone else wanted to say anything to her.

My aunt said, "She seems to be breathing slower. Maybe you should check her oxygen line and make sure it's not kinked." I assured her that it wasn't kinked, but that she was in her last few minutes of life.

My grandmother stared as if in a trance. My cousin looked at my mom and dropped his head. No one spoke.

In the silence, I leaned in and told her, "I'm going to miss you, but I know it's time for you to go. I asked God to let me be here when you transitioned, and I'm here. You can let go. It's okay. I'll see you in Paradise at the appointed time."

She breathed three erratic breaths and fell silent. It was 8:54 pm, February 16, 2009. I was numb for two years.

7

Relinquishing Mom

This world is not my home. I'm just a passing thru.
My treasures are laid up somewhere beyond the blue.
The angels beckon me from Heaven's open door,
And I can't feel at home in this world anymore.

I went through the motions of managing my mom's homegoing service with achy bones, splitting head, and white blood cell count through the floor. It was my responsibility to send her home in style.

Fortunately, we had already sketched out her 16-page 8" x 11" program book. I only needed to secure the

The loss of either parent would have cut me deeply, but my mother shaped my life like no one else: what I served for dinner (or didn't), who I married (or divorced), the work I chose (or had forced upon me).

57

tributes from her children, husband, and mother, but they were too grief stricken. This left me with three empty pages. Well, she wasn't going to be looking at me from Heaven with stink eye! So I wrote them.

My dad's:

Baby

"Baby" and "My wife" are a couple of endearments I used when referring to you. I had a couple others, but since this reading is for public viewing, I won't include those here.

You brought so much joy and happiness to my life. When I first met you, you were a young woman with three beautiful children. I have to admit that I was skeptical about getting married into a ready-made family. However, after our five-year long courtship, God pointed me in the direction I should go. I knew that you were the woman I was supposed to marry and to be with for the rest of my life. Baby, you are the love of my life.

After we were married you gave me another child, and although in her younger years people teased and said you could never deny me as her father, she has grown to look more and more like you.

We've been through some tough financial times, but God always supplied our needs. And when food was scarce, you could turn one chicken, some green beans and corn, and some brown-and-serve rolls into a king's feast! You always made sure we ate as a family, and there is no one in the world who can cook like you … and look so good doing it. You were beautiful in every way.

We were together so long. I wish I could say

we never argued, but we did. Sometimes it was my fault, sometimes yours ... OK, maybe it was more my fault than yours, but through those times we grew stronger, loved harder, and respected each other more deeply.

You were an excellent mother and a shining example to our girls. Our sons had something to aspire to when they considered selecting a wife. I walked tall every time you were on my arm. I look back at photos taken of us, and I had an air of "Yes, I'm all that" about me, because you were beside me and you were mine. You had a strut about you that would make any woman envious and any man swoon.

We've faced some difficult times when difficult decisions had to be made, and you were a woman of virtue and of valor. You made the tough decisions and the right decisions for our family. Even though you honored me as the head of the house, some things I simply deferred to you because you were right.

I have to admit I have a very unique character. Some have even called me crazy. But in my mind, I couldn't be crazy, because I had you. How could someone so beautiful, intelligent, talented, and artistic be in love with a crazy person? All I can say is if I am crazy, crazy got me you, therefore, crazy must be good!

Baby, you managed to raise four beautiful and successful children, worked for the federal government in a coveted position for over 30 years, preached the word of God and won souls for Christ, and made me the happiest man on Earth, all without breaking a sweat. You have given me wonderful memories for a lifetime. You were the example of Christ-like behavior that caused me to give my life to the Lord. The thought of you being in Paradise awaiting Christ's return will be ever present in my mind to keep me on the straight and narrow so that we will meet again.

My heart fluttered when I first laid eyes on you. Your presence and your touch comforted me throughout our lifetime together, and even in your transition, your presence ignited me because of your perpetual beauty, strength, and courage. You have given me a lifetime of love, happiness, and support. I rejoice with you as you rejoice in Heaven, because God has restored you to your place of dancing with praise, singing with victory, and worshiping in spirit and in truth.

Until we meet again,
Your Loving Husband, Warner

Mom's children's:

A Mother Like No Other

Mom, you were truly extraordinary in your demeanor, your beauty, your talent, and your love. We have many summertime memories when the back door was open and the kitchen window was open and you were at the sink cleaning greens. We were outside playing while you prepared a multi-course meal from scratch. Then, lo and behold, we heard you singing a hymn, your angelic voice strong and fervent as if you were sitting at the feet of Jesus. Because your voice was so strong and could be heard practically by the entire neighborhood, we as kids stood frozen wondering what in the world our friends would think. When they said, "Who is that? It's beautiful," we let out a sigh of relief, puffed out our chests as wide as they could go, and cheesed from ear to ear. "That's my mom. Oh, she sings like that all the time." Those were good times—good stuff.

We can never forget the many times we've gone out with you and people have asked, "Is that your sister?" Rodney missed out on a number of potential girlfriends because you were mistaken as "his girl." Of course I got the, "Man, that's your MOM? I know you hope you look like that when you grow up!" When one of my girlfriends made that statement, it was OK. When it was a potential boyfriend, I wasn't too happy with you at the moment. Alicia didn't have as many moments like that because she was gorgeous as well. And with Richard, he really wasn't fazed by too much.

You had a way of turning a simple family gathering into a world class banquet. Our living room would be converted into a dining hall with tablecloths, china, and crystal. Of course we sat at the kids table, but that didn't matter. The transformation in itself was something to behold. You never complained about the many days of preparation required to make EVERYTHING from scratch. You would smile and sing as you prepared and be so happy with the finished product that the house would be all abuzz with excitement just from watching you. And when the day arrived and everyone was gathered at the house, every room completely filled with people and food, you would be the perfect hostess. You filled the house with laughter as only you could, your shoulders bouncing up and down, the most beautiful smile on your face. Wow, you were truly amazing.

There were so many little unforgettable things you would do: the way you would eat a plate of greens with your fingers orchestrating a dance from the cornbread to the collards to your mouth without dropping a crumb; the way you drank a glass of ice cold water (from YOUR special glass) as if you were standing in the middle of the Sahara Desert; the way you would suck on a mint as if it were your last meal; the way you chewed grapes and sniffed at the same time because smelling your food helped you to taste it better; the way you had your own tambourine (in its own case) and played it like no one on this entire Earth; the way your face would light up when you preached; the way you would flick your hair off your shoulder when it got good to you as if to clear the way for the next powerful word; and, we can't forget, the way you did the cutest yet most sincere and anointed dance in church, even with three and four inch heels!

Mom you were great, gorgeous, giving, talented, tenacious, terrific, beautiful, bold, benevolent, caring, courteous, and captivating. Now you are free to walk around Heaven, free of oxygen tanks, breathing normally, rejoicing as your heart desires, and again singing like an angel as you give God all the praise and all the honor.

We love you so much and will hold you close in our hearts,

Alicia, Rodney, Richard, and Sheri

My Grandmother's:

My Precious Little Brownie

Brownie, you are my first born child, the one that has been with me the longest. I was still but a child myself when I had you, so in some ways we grew up together and became the best of friends. I knew when you were just a few days old that you were a fighter with a strong will (that's a very polite way of saying "stubborn"). But that's alright because that stubbornness caused you to not let go in difficult times when others would have simply walked away. When the odds seemed to be formidably set against you, you knew where your help came from—the Lord.

All of my children are talented, but you were my little songbird. God anointed your voice and you could bring a congregation to its feet before you made it through the first verse of song. There are some people who have talent but don't appreciate or enjoy it; but you loved to sing and God honored that. As the oldest, you held the honor of the first-born, but you also held the responsibility, and you lived up to it very well.

In addition to singing, there was something else that you really enjoyed doing and that was eating. God truly blessed you with good metabolism, because you should have been big as a house—I mean a mansion, as much as you loved to eat. Instead, you always had the cutest little figure. I can remember times when you were pregnant and I would cook up a kitchen full of food. Just when I thought you couldn't possibly eat anymore, you would. Greens, cornbread, fried apple pies, smothered chicken, fried cabbage, catfish, and the list goes on. You ate it all and enjoyed it!

You were a beautiful little girl with the prettiest smile and gorgeous bright brown eyes. Then you blossomed into this beautiful woman, a woman who gave me four beautiful and respectful grandchildren; a virtuous woman with strong family values; a saved, sanctified and Holy Ghost filled woman who could preach like the Apostle Paul; a woman who loved and honored her parents; and a woman who was obedient to the will of God.

Brownie, you made me proud. Our relationship was unique and special. I was with you through many tough spots in your life, holding you in my arms, comforting you and praying for you. You brought me joy and brought us closer and built a bond between us that can never be broken.

God allowed me to bring you into this world and when He decided it was time for you to return home to Him, I was there right beside you. You can again rejoice freely, praise Him wholeheartedly, and dance like you've never danced before. I rejoice in your deliverance, and I praise God for your peace.

I will always love you and thank God for the time He gave you to me.

Forever Your Mommy,
The Honorable Prophetess Dr. Hattie B. Jones

The loss of either parent would have cut me deeply, but my mother shaped my life like no one else: what I served for dinner (or didn't), who I married (or divorced), the work I chose (or had forced upon me). Those things taught me what it meant to be a woman. Whether I modeled my choices on hers or cringed at the very thought, whether I nurtured or neglected the girl I really was (as opposed to the one she thought I would be), my mother was my North Star.

While she lit my way, she also linked me to the past. It was Mom who kept the baby book and handed down Grandma's stories along with the heirloom china. As Hope Edelman pointed out in her book, *Motherless Daughters*, such family legends "transform the experiences of [a woman's] female ancestors into maps she can follow for warning or encouragement."

As a bereaved daughter, I have talked about my "mommy hunger." It made me wish that an older, wiser friend would adopt me. It sent a pang of envy through me at the sight of a mother and daughter laughing together over lunch. A friend, during the first year after her mother's death, couldn't fall asleep without hugging a pillow. Another kept her mother's hospital bed silk robe a decade later. In my own bottom bathroom drawer has sat my mother's hairbrush and comb, which I have used every day for more than five years after her death. Using her comb and brush has taken me back to her cinnamon-scented kitchen, where she gave me her perspective of my triumphs and tragedies.

Beyond following her beauty regimen, I found myself doing what she did. I mourned hard and slowly. I learned to accept the yearning that blindsided me when something wonderful happened and she wasn't around to share it.

After a while I found myself breaking new ground. When I saw women my age chatting with their mothers over lunch, I wished them many more outings together. When I'd hear that a woman lost her mother, I'd be the one to write a note this time, to offer my help on her path to her mother's empty house. I have found no better way to honor my mother.

And then there was the completely unexpected change: maturation. From as early as I can remember, I looked forward to certain milestones that would switch my status to big girl, and later to all grown-up. There was the first day of school, the mastery of long division, the first bra, the first date, graduation, turning 21, the first full-time job, and, should all else fail, that surefire marker of adulthood, marriage. I climbed the life ladder at a steady pace, as did most of my friends, but well into our 20s and 30s, when careers and/or families had been established, we would still occasionally confide to one another, "You know, I don't really feel grown-up." Approaching 40, I speculated that this was perhaps one of the best-kept secrets of life.

Then, all too suddenly, I grew up. The events that catapulted me over the barrier to my own maturity were the unanticipated sickness and death of my mother, coupled with my own battle with cancer and a near death experience. Tragedy did it.

Slowly, a new me emerged, one that could lay claim to the status of grown-up. Central to that new self was a vivid, visceral knowledge of my own mortality. My expectation of a likely life span shrank from a wishful 99 (the age of my maternal great grandmother at her death) to 67 (the age of my mom at her death). At 41, after surviving the whole chest pain fiasco, I began to feel I was living on borrowed time.

Time became a gift, which I received with both gladness and a degree of guilt. The hard reality is that not everyone survives the fight, and I would often asked, "Why me and not them?"

As the predictive mathematical power of my mortality waned, an awareness of life's vulnerability and uncertainty rose. Death embedded deep in me a knowledge of my limit, human limits. Oddly, that felt like the beginning of maturity. A strange milestone.

For a while that knowledge separated me from many friends of my age. A few years later, though, I was far less alone in my losses. A single death had transformed our lives, age and nature of the relationship aside.

Death steals:

"Mom."

"Mom?"

"Mom!"

Save surrogates, it steals that word forever.

"Your mom ... she died," are words too big to fit any ears. They are a swinging wrecking ball inside your head coming at you again and again until, finally, they crack your brain and split you apart.

Research has shown that grief is keenest within the first six months of parental loss, but it was in the following years that I achieved a new emotional equilibrium. It took years to unfold the deeper, lasting consequences of being motherless. Sadly, less research was available to prepare me for that.

After her death everything changed a bit inside of me. Acquainting myself with the new internal me certainly drove some external changes, but it was the internal changes that seemed simultaneously more important and harder to explain. The seriousness. My mortal conscious.

It was like when I was a little girl and I chose my own outfit for the day for the first time ... within her guidelines. *Will she like this?* Even if her answer would be, "Heck no!" my choice to wear or not to wear was with her in mind.

After her death I didn't ask any longer. I was on my own. The pressure was off in some ways but on in others. Now I had to answer to myself.

I've realized in retrospect that it was my mom's death that changed me, more so than battling breast cancer at 40. The breast cancer focused my energies, but the loss of my mother unleashed my activism.

The shedding of ill-fitting maternal expectations, the luxury of separating myself a bit, led to new career paths, a more sympathetic and appreciative understanding of her, and even a clarity about transference of insecurities: "Well, it was okay for her to feel that way, and so maybe it's okay for me to feel the same way." Fresh eyes helped me to see her as the center of her life, not the arbiter of mine. I had become an adult.

Research has shown that in the United States, most people have lost their mothers between the ages of 45 and 64. Popular wisdom and psychological convention have identified that same season as the time when most people have increased reflection, taken stock, and initiated change, often called the midlife crisis. That's how it happened for me.

Mom was the connective tissue to that world that, had she not left, I would never have left. I suspect life would have been softer and more certain if Mom had lived, but it has become more expansive, independent, and interesting, for which I'm grateful. It's when I've done something beyond what she dreamed that I miss her the most.

Perhaps the impact of my mother's death on me was unusually strong because our generations spanned opposite sides of the cultural divide carved by the women's movement, beyond the natural tug-of-war between generations. When she died, so did the tug of her generational and personal values if they had not become authentically my own. That sudden slackening of that rope was disorienting at first, then liberating, and eventually enlightening. Roaming untethered, I have seen her from more objective vantage points and constructed a far more encompassing image of her essence.

The untethering released me to write this book. I would not have revealed all of our generational differences otherwise. The untethering allowed me to choose where I reattached to her values. In her absence, I have become more like her domestic, nurturing self. That and other qualities I have tried to replace have enlarged me, and gratitude has abounded from that growth. How exciting it has been to think of my dear Yvonne as the center of her life as I am of mine.

8

Grieving

Life went on. That was tricky.

July 2, 2009

I'm still here!!!

Today I completed the last of 33 radiation treatments, and I am ecstatic. I still have some complications I'm dealing with—scar tissue, swelling, low white blood cell count, and a pending bone marrow biopsy—but my treatments are complete! I'm learning to accept my complications as subtle reminders of the bigger blessings I've experienced this year.

I couldn't experience real joy if I couldn't feel sorrow, nor could I find happiness if I was busy running from sadness.

I hope that during this time of support for me that you have learned more about the power of prayer, God's love and miracle working power, and the real value of true friends' and family's love. If you didn't, shame on you, because I certainly did!!

Love, peace, and good health to all,

Sheri

You are the embodiment of inspiration and power through believing!
Kay

10-06-09
Hey everybody,

October 1st made one year since I discovered my breast cancer. Some of you were aware that I had another biopsy on October 1st. This time it was a bone marrow biopsy. I got the results back, and, thank God, I do not have leukemia or lymphoma.

I wish I could say that I've been "stronger than ever," but I haven't. Last year this time, Mom was with me through the diagnosis. This past week, I was facing another potential cancer diagnosis without her. Yes, I talked to her and, yes, I know that a part of her lives in me. I used to talk to my mom all the time, sometimes three times on bad days. I don't have that anymore, so it's not the same. When I think of her suffering, I'm so thankful that God delivered her and called her home, but that selfish part of me came to the surface this past week. I wanted her here.

Love to you all,
Sheri

Dear Sheri,

Sweet daughter of mine, I too am so glad that IT'S NOT CANCER!!!!! I sorely miss your Mom not being around for both of us, but she told me before she left this world that life must go on.

Keep your head up, Sheri. We will get through this together. Know that whenever you need me, I'll be here for you. I am always only a phone call away.

Love forever,
Daddy

I had to almost immediately get back into my daily routine. I expected my children to need me functioning at a high level right away, but I was startled by how quickly others wanted me to get back to the business of passing out my resources as usual. It felt as crass as that.

As long as I have experienced success, I have shared and helped others in need. That ethic lined up with my two-year-old declaration to be a helper. It didn't matter, though, that I was managing grief and waging my own fight against death of body and mind. The people who needed help didn't hesitate to ask.

That first request was surreal. It was as if she didn't notice my missing limb and blood pouring. The requests were nothing new, but honestly! Some people needed a little sensitivity training.

It made the mourning harder to bear when it seemed that nobody understood. If it felt like that when everyone knew how close my mother and I were, I couldn't imagine how "disenfranchised grief" felt.

Disenfranchised grief is the pain of a significant loss that is not openly acknowledged or socially supported. Often people suffer that pain in isolation. Kenneth J. Doka, PhD, the professor of gerontology at the College of New Rochelle in New York coined the term in 1985 and gave these examples:

- An ex-husband passes away and your friends don't see why it matters.

- An executive is having a serious affair with her married co-worker; when he dies, she can't say, "He was the love of my life."

∾ A gay person's partner becomes ill, but they've never been open about their relationship.

In some cases, society doesn't consider the loss a tragedy. (A beloved pet is killed; an adult sibling dies.) In other cases, it's unacceptable for *you* to feel badly. (Your child is diagnosed with a mental disability, and you're not supposed to have or vocalize any disappointment.) In other cases, the death may produce shame and fear of judgment. (A family member commits suicide or dies of AIDS.)

The problem with suffering in silence is that you don't have support when you need it most, says Mary McCambridge, a New York-based grief counselor and founder of the Foundation for Grieving Children. She explains that bottling up intense feelings often leads to deep resentment and is stressful on the body, which can make you more vulnerable to illness.

How many times had I held it in during my lifetime? How deeply was I falling victim again as other people's needs overrode my need to catch my breath?

I had to find people who would understand. I had to learn to be honest about how I felt. I had to recognize that there was nothing wrong with me, and that whatever my feelings were, they were legitimate. I didn't choose grief, but there it was with all of its pain and emotional turmoil. I had to go through it, and I was much healthier when I claimed my right to do it. It ended up being one of the most difficult—and important—things I had ever experienced, and not just for the obvious reasons.

Learning how to cope was crucial to getting through the difficult times. The ways I chose to cope shaped other important dimensions of my life, like how much meaning and satisfaction I found rather than with what kind of chronic problems I would contend. Facing the awful feelings increased my capacity to experience the feelings that make life worth living. Unfortunately, that was easier said than done, even when I had learned how.

I had not had many opportunities to practice using that coping skill before now. In fact, like most people, I had done just the opposite: I got over painful personal situations and didn't let my feelings pester me or anyone else. Avoiding my feelings in my grief could have led me to medicate as so many do with drugs, alcohol, etc.

Instead, I developed a ritual to commemorate my mom's passing, visiting her grave when I could take as much time as I needed to express my anguish. In that one decision, I opened the door for learning to care for me.

Grieving was not really about handling *losses* at all, although the fact that it helped me to do that was a welcome bonus. Grieving was about handling *myself* when I was facing difficult situations. Each stage of the grieving process involved doing things I *needed* to do to provide myself with the same open, compassionate, and supportive response I provided to others when something bad happened to them. Difficulties arose only when I somehow got stuck in one stage of the process.

Experts who study the grieving process nailed my experience in their identification of the five major stages of grief:

1. **Denial or numbness.** From disbelief to complete emotional shutdown (which made it appear as if I wasn't affected at all), grief prompted self-defense measures to protect me from experiencing the full intensity of the loss all at once. Periods of denial and numbness alternated with my acknowledgement of what happened, its implications, and the feelings that came with it.

2. **Anger.** At many points, I got angry. I felt abandoned. My mother's absence was causing so much pain and difficulty. I couldn't fix her. Anger prevented me from feeling overwhelmed, debilitated, and powerless.

3. **Bargaining.** With nearly two decades of medical practice, I had plenty of information to keep me preoccupied with how I could have prevented her death. If ... if ...if. If I had bought her a softer pillow ... Even if I figured out the anatomical links to a cure, it would be too late for her to benefit. All of this thinking kept powerful feelings at arm's length when I needed them, but I also drew lessons from the situation.

4. **Depression.** Definitely. I had the symptoms. Difficulty sleeping. Loss of appetite. It took extra determination to meet day-to-day

responsibilities. I was certainly less social. That temporary withdrawal of energy from external affairs was necessary for me to have the time and opportunity to reorganize my emotional life to match my new reality.

5. **Acceptance.** At some point, I was able to integrate what had happened and all my feelings and reactions into my "life-story," allowing Mom's death to take its appropriate place alongside other significant experiences. This did *not* mean that I was "done" with the loss. I didn't move on as if it never happened. It simply didn't dominate my mental and emotional landscape.

For me, grief happened in intermingled stages and come and go behaviors, none of it right or wrong, none according to a prescribed timetable. Once I had been through it, I became pretty clear about when I'd go through it again and again. It wouldn't take a major loss such as a death, serious illness, or loss of an important relationship or object to set the grieving process in motion. Any significant change could ignite the stages, including positive ones like having a child finish school and move out, getting a better job, reaching a weight loss goal, or suddenly realizing I wasn't quite the same person I used to be. Every life change entailed a loss of what used to be (or what might have been), a transition into something new. I learned to recognize that strange position of grieving for something I *wanted* to change.

One of the biggest challenges in my grief experience was not getting stuck in a certain stage. That usually happened when my old belief system told me that a "good" person wouldn't have the feelings or thoughts I was having. "It's not right," I'd tell myself, "to feel numb or detached after something terrible happened, to be angry at someone who died or got sick, to feel guilty about something we had no control over, or to get so depressed I couldn't meet my responsibilities." Or, in other grief experiences, I'd feel foolish for feeling sad about losing something I didn't like very much anyway. When I found myself having those feelings, I'd fight them. In the process, I made the feelings stronger, made myself feel worse, and diminished my ability to participate in the natural process of integrating the loss into my life.

My feelings were not bad or wrong. My pain was worth acknowledgement. Facing everything I felt was exactly what I needed to do to accept and heal my wounds, which might never have quite gone away.

There were times when my feelings seemed too overwhelming to allow me to function as I needed to, so I set aside specific times every day to allow whatever feelings I had to come up. In essence, I stopped fighting my feelings and let myself express them physically. I actively grieved and mourned. Grief was the inner sense; mourning was my outward expression. So I cried, shouted, and screamed, and sometimes hid in my closet when I needed to get away from people.

Emotions were designed to move me to do something. If I had left out the "doing something" part, I would not have fully expressed the feeling. I was cautious that no one was on the receiving end of my hurt. I also saved my expressions until I was not around anyone who might be inclined to call the police, because I was acting a little strangely!

Perhaps my biggest revelation was recognizing that times of grief were not the times to play superhero. I wasn't able to function at my best, so I accepted all the help I could get. I looked to loved ones and others for support. I spent time alone, which was fine, but I limited it because isolation wasn't healthy. Sometimes when I needed to scream to the mountain tops or when the tears would flow, my support came from the most unexpected places. Then expected supporters, e.g., certain people in my family, scolded or silenced me, saying things like, "Keep it together. People are watching you and counting on you to be strong."

Even at my mother's bedside, moments after she died, I felt the rush of intense loss consuming me. When my tears gushed, a family member said, "Shh, keep yourself together."

I should have told this person, "Have you lost your mind! My mother is dead!" but I didn't. I did as I was told; I did what I "had to do." In retrospect, I regret it because doing so prolonged my grieving process, making it that much more difficult.

I emerged from my grief with the knowledge of a simple truth. My positive and negative feelings were one "package." I couldn't experience real joy if I couldn't feel sorrow, nor could I find happiness if I was busy running from sadness. The amount of pleasure and meaning I got from my relationships was directly proportional to my capacity to feel the pain of loneliness. I could only know of the pride of my accomplishments if I endured the anxiety of taking risks or the shame of failing.

When Mom died, it was my turn to take the risk and feel that dagger in the heart. The philosopher Nietzsche said that what doesn't kill us makes us stronger. That held very true for my grieving, but only when I let myself work with—not against—*all* the feelings and thoughts that came as a result.

As a doctor, I have seen people with chronic, life-threatening illnesses struggle with death and dying. I have also seen families struggle with the inevitable end of life, families who weren't truly prepared for the avalanche of emotions that swept over them when the final moment came, even when they knew death was imminent. I now knew how challenging and devastating the raw, intense emotions of grief could be, because it had happened to me. I had also experienced love in its capacity to lift burdens off the heart of humanity, turn duty into delight, and change even sorrow to joy.

As painful as my own grief was, it gave me new insight on dealing with theirs. I understood how grief clouded my ability to make sound decisions and consumed significant amounts of my energy. I learned not to make any major decisions during that time, such as moving, major financial changes, or relationships.

So many people kept telling me that things would get better in time, and to an extent, they were right.

Time does help, but it might not cure. Time was able to make that acute, searing pain of loss less intense and to make my red-hot emotions less painful, but my feelings of loss and emptiness never completely went away. Expecting time to "fix it" created a false anticipation, which I should have taken with a measure of caution.

Accepting and embracing my new "normal" helped me reconcile my losses. The accompanying self-reflection and personal growth I experienced was extraordinary. It helped me to master emotional intelligence in my medical practice. Emotional intelligence is defined by Salovey and Mayer as "the ability to perceive and express emotion, assimilate emotion in thought, understand and reason with emotion, and regulate emotion in the self and others."[1]

There was little discussion of emotional intelligence in my medical practice and medical education, the core competencies of emotional intelligence being the perception of emotions (in oneself and others), the understanding of these emotions, and the management of emotions. Perception of emotions required that I as the physician be more "mindful" in the practice of medicine and in my daily life.[2] As a mindful physician, I was to note the sadness, fear, joy, anger, regret, and other emotions that inevitably arose in my day-to-day practice. Only by becoming aware of

---

1   Salovey P, Mayer JD. *Emotional intelligence. Imagination, Cognition, and Personality* 1990; 9: 185-211.

2   Epstein RM. *Mindful Practice*. JAMA 1999; 282: 833-839. [PubMed]

those emotions, then, could I seek to understand and manage them in a way that would promote personal and professional growth.

By the very nature of my work, I often had profound, moving, and sometimes disturbing experiences, but the most recent ones hit me like a ton of bricks. Those experiences have catalyzed my personal growth, but growth only occurred because I took the time to reflect on the experience, process its implications for my personal and professional development, and initiated behavior change. Reflection promoted a deeper understanding of myself and others.

Part of the reason I became a physician was because I got tired of simply watching those close to me suffer through illness and eventually die while I helplessly stood by, unable to do anything. Throughout my medical training I watched as my mentors interacted with their patients, displaying a political correctness matched with just enough outward emotion that there was no telling the difference between the good news and the bad. It boggled my mind how callous many of my mentors could be when delivering the news of impending death to patients and their family. Although they did not wish death upon them, nor could they do anything to change the outcome, couldn't they *care*? Couldn't they go an extra step to show that they cared whether they lived or died?

During my residency I skipped lunch (literally, the only time I had to myself) to spend extra time with my critically ill patients. During this time my patients could address issues that were not strictly medical.

Some would discuss a divorce brought on by the devastation of their diseases, a child's wedding they expected to miss, or the upcoming birth of a grandchild that their impending death would certainly prevent them from experiencing. Many times, I would wind up in tears or giving an embrace.

I believe that my crying stemmed from being "very involved" in my cases, which led me to "take everything to heart." This was the start of emotional intelligence for me. I realized that this level of involvement was uncommon, but I believed that I could not be any other kind of doctor. I'd always been a very emotional person.

"Don't let your emotions get too involved" and "Never take those feelings home with you" were things I heard often during my training, which worked in theory. However, I endured the ordeal with the patients; in a sense, I became part of the family. So as much as I respected my mentors, I let those words go in one ear and out the other. I treated every patient as if she or he were a member of my family. When that patient became my mom, I realized more than ever that the more I walked in truth, obedience, and empathy, the more my feelings cooperated and prodded me in the right direction. Loving my mom in life and death reminded me of why I went into medicine in the first place.

There was no better feeling than watching a patient who entered my life with one foot in the coffin walk out of the hospital on his own two feet. Sometimes it took days, sometimes it took months, but there came a point where my treatment transcended medicine. I have prayed with the families, encouraged my patients, and instilled hope in everyone that anything is possible.

On the other hand, there was no greater pain than losing a patient without an adequate explanation, whether it was an elderly lady whose life I spent a month saving only to have her suddenly pass away days before her scheduled release or a young healthy female who walked into the hospital with a seemingly common problem who failed to survive surgery. It never got any easier to deal with the loss. Complications happened, and they could happen to anyone, but I never expected them to end like that.

I didn't always have the answers why, and that's what I hated the most. Sometimes I found myself in my pre-medical school days standing by helplessly. The shock left me at a loss for words. When I was a young doctor, I sat down with a terminal lung cancer patient and her husband to discuss the woman's gloomy prognosis. She cried, he cried, and I cried; it was an unforgettable moment in all of our lives.

What did I do when I didn't know what to do? My strength and resources may have been gone, but my empathy would be ever present, guiding my patient to a level of peace that only came from knowing they were not alone and that someone cared and understood their pain, fear, and loss.

My patients didn't think I lacked emotions or suppressed them to do my job professionally. I celebrated lives that were saved, and I grieved and mourned those that were lost. Sometimes I took grief home with me.

I would always caution friends and family that doctors have bad days, get depressed, get sick, can be as irrational as patients, can be forgetful, can miss the obvious, can get distracted, can get annoyed by our kids, can fail at marriage, can experience trauma, and can be irritable from a difficult appointment. As the patient, though, more often than not I didn't naturally think about any of those things when my appointment time came to see a doctor. In my mind, their lives couldn't have been all that bad; after all, they were working, were healthy, and didn't have cancer. I had to make a conscious effort to *see* and *feel* my doctors as the human beings they were and not as the role or title they carried and not as robots in a perfect world. Far from it. Sometimes things wouldn't go as I thought they should. That was when trusting in God's sovereignty was essential.

Regardless of what side of the table I was on, patient's or physician's or both, I realized that my stressful situations had purpose. I believed that God was more interested in changing me than He was in changing my circumstances. He wanted me to get to the point where I was content, not disturbed or dissatisfied, regardless of my circumstance. When I was content, even if my circumstances changed, I didn't spin out in distress, causing me to be distracted from living like Christ.

One day, the sun did shine again. I didn't realize it at first. My days became brighter and my life went on, even though it would never be quite the same.

9
New Life

I only missed three days of work in 10 months of treatment, and most people never knew what I was going through. People had no idea about me losing my hair, half of a breast, my mom, and my marriage. They didn't know the toll it was having on my psyche. The ones who did know didn't know what to say or do about it. I determined to share my story with my patients and co-workers on a need-to-know basis and put it all behind me.

In the summer of 2010, two significant events occurred. The first was that I participated in my first my first Susan G. Komen 3-Day event in Chicago. The love and compassion I felt as a survivor in that environment was indescribable. I was surrounded by thousands of people who

My problems have not completely disappeared, but my attitude and response to them have made all the difference, both for myself and for others.

shared my goal of a world without breast cancer. It was life changing.

Shortly after that I experienced another life changing event: Lymphedema set in. The lymph nodes in my right arm were destroyed between the surgery and radiation, which caused permanent and at times colossal swelling in my right arm, hand, and fingers. The swelling made performing the clinical aspects of my job impossible.

To add insult to injury, my boss at that time, who was not a physician, told me, "A physician who is not clinically capable is of no value to me." Having been born and raised on the Southside of Chicago, I should have cussed him out and told him where he and his entire family, including his mama, could go. But I couldn't. Not because of my moral high ground, but because I was crushed. At 42, after all of this suffering, I had no value.

After eight weeks of daily physical and occupational therapy, I sent an email:

Oct 4, 2010
Hi Everyone,

I haven't sent an update in a while, because I wanted to share as much information as possible. My lymphedema has progressed to a point that I have required intensive physical and occupational therapy. After 5 weeks of therapy, I have not improved. Last Wednesday I had a lymphoscintigraphy (the most painful test I have ever had in my entire life!!!). It demonstrated that there is no lymphatic activity in my right upper extremity. A renowned specialist relegated me to see a pain specialist for

treatment of post radiation pain syndrome, continued physical therapy, lymphatic draining, massage
5 days a week, and banding 7 days a week, 22 hours
per day for the next six weeks. Then, we'll see. Not
the news I wanted to share.

On my two-year cancer-free anniversary, I'm
still battling the effects of this disease. It has
changed every aspect of my life. I wanted to move
on, but God obviously has me in a holding pattern.
Please continue to keep me in your prayers. Despite
my disappointment and changes in my life physically, mentally and financially, my ultimate desire
is to be in the will of God so that His purpose can
be demonstrated in my life and so that I can do the
work that He had planned for me long ago.

God Bless,
Sheri, Dr. P, DivaMD

Two very endearing responses were these:

Sheri,

I'm sorry that you're still facing so many challenges,
but grateful that God is still leading you through. My husband, Eric, was just asking about you last night, and I told
him I hadn't heard from you in a while. I told him today
about your email, and his question was, "Is she still 'fine'?"
I said that you gave no indication otherwise, and he said,
"Well, then she's still all good!" Fortunately, although he's
obviously been drooling over you since he met you, I know
you, and so I won't be jealous. Anyone else, and they'd
have to go on my list, and it's not a list you want to be on!

Anyway, keep the faith.
Liane

Goodness gracious – you continue to amaze me. I am so sorry to hear about your struggles, and discomfort and pain. You don't deserve that. You're such an incredible woman….but I do believe God doesn't give us more than we can handle, and He's certainly proving how strong you are. I love your faith. You are such a role model for me. I try so hard to stay hope-filled, and get so easily frustrated, then there you are – just moving right along and praying to do God's will so hard I have no doubt God is holding you gently (because tight would hurt) and His plans for you are perfect!

Know I love you and you're in my prayers. If I can do anything at all, please do not hesitate to ask.

Linda

Over the next few months, I endured daily physical therapy, my boss terminated me from my executive management position from an organization from which I thought I would someday retire, and I began wearing my compression garments 22/7. Now considered disabled from clinical practice, I set out to reinvent myself to stabilize myself financially. After careful consideration, I decided to spend my lifetime sharing my story, sharing my life, and fighting to bring an end to this disease. I had no idea how that would translate into putting food on the table for my two teenagers who expected to eat every day! I knew, though, that doing so would bring me sheer joy. That revelation came in December 2010.

The following January, Susan G. Komen put out a national call to all past participants from 2007 to that point. They were looking for a new National Spokesperson. The subject line of the email read, "Could you be the next National Spokesperson for Susan G. Komen 3-Day?" Out of hundreds of applications, they offered the position to me and I gladly accepted.

I was honored to represent the Susan G. Komen 3-Day as the National Spokesperson. The role afforded me the opportunity to raise awareness and educate thousands of women and men throughout the country about breast health and how they could join in the fight to end breast cancer. I went from being diagnosed with breast cancer in 2008 to being disabled by lymphedema in 2010 to being the Susan G. Komen 3-Day National Spokesperson in 2011. Now that's living!

That uncaring and single-minded boss helped me receive the revelation that my value was not found in my "do" but in my "who." I was valuable. God said so. God had a great plan for my life. I was going to live it out.

My friend Dan once said this:

At some point during the battle, God-fearing or not, we all have a cross that feels like it's more than we can bear. It's only when we carry it that our limits are tested, broken, redefined, and rebuilt. Every single one of us has, at some point, given in. I recently talked with an absolute powerhouse named Dr. Sheri who, instead of calling 911 for her chest pains, went to sleep thinking, "If this is how I'm going out, so be it, because God, I'm just so tired of fighting." And when she woke up, her limits were tested ... broken ... redefined ... and would eventually be rebuilt.

On a daily basis I began to take steps, no matter how small, to break the patterns of my past. I refused to live in fear of a recurrence, new cancer, or metastases. My life-long dream of being a practicing physician was stripped from me in an instant, and admittedly I wanted to die as I saw no hope. I thought the world would not miss me or my talents and it might even be better off without me. Stepping past my fear opened a flood of blessings I could have never imagined. God was guiding my footsteps, leading me into a career and life that was full. Sometimes I felt as if I could burst.

With the limited time I had on Earth, not because of any illness, but because I'm human, I would ask myself daily, "What am I doing with my time?" I would answer, "I'm changing my outlook. I'm looking to a new way of doing things. I'm accepting a new vision. I'm renewing my faith and trust in The One."

Joy didn't come from having my circumstances in order or under control; it came from what was in my heart. Contentment was not about fame, how much money I had, my position at work, my social standing, my education, or the side of the tracks where I was born. It was about my heart attitude. The happiest people I knew were truly thankful and truly content, meaning satisfied and undisturbed no matter what was going on, which was different from complacent.

I wanted things to get better, and I believed that

God was working and things were changing. I have seen the result in due time. My problems have not completely disappeared, but my attitude and response to them have made all the difference, both for myself and for others.

After my diagnoses and the death of my mother, I faced the harsh reality that I had spent the first half of my life merely existing. Since reconciling my loss and subsequently all that I have gained, I have decided to LIVE!

> Love myself and others
> Inspire those around me
> Voice my dreams
> Enjoy life

I L.I.V.E. every day, and as a result I will leave behind a legacy that will hopefully allow others to journey along a path that is not as harsh, not as lonely, and not nearly as painful.

Epilogue

Back in high school, I was on the pep squad all four years. I had the opportunity to get to know all of the basketball and football players, because I cheered at all of the games. Our school was known for having some of the smartest students on our teams, but they weren't the best players, so we didn't win many games. They were college bound and very sweet on the eyes. Because of that, it was very lovely to practice at the same time that the football team practiced. At one particular practice during my sophomore year, a new player walked out on the field, and OH MY WORD. He was a 6'3", lean, thick and curly haired bundle of café au lait goodness! After some investigative maneuvers on my part, I discovered that he was a senior. Only one year to get him to notice me.

I didn't.

Mr. au Lait smiled and spoke when he saw me at games, practice, or in the hallways, but otherwise not a move did he make. Although I was born and raised in Chicago, I was very much reared in the southern way. I certainly was NOT going to be the one to make the first move. He graduated and I went on with my life as an upper classman.

Two years later I graduated and matriculated at

Northwestern University. During my first quarter, lo and behold, Mr. Café au Lait walked into my dorm. Yep, the fine football player who never gave me any play in high school. I thought surely he would notice me now. After all, we lived in the same dorm, this was college, and many guys found light-skinned, green-eyed, intelligent young ladies with brown hair flowing down their backs quite attractive.

He didn't notice me!

For two years, he never made a move. He always spoke and smiled and even held the door for me a couple of times, but alas that would be all the play I got. He graduated and I went on with my life as an upper classman.

When I got to Loyola Stritch School of Medicine, I was one of only two minority students in the entire class of 132—one black female and one black male. Since the minority community at Loyola was quite small, we always looked out for each other. We came from all over the country with no history between us, yet we became fast friends out of necessity.

I remember one day during my fourth year helping a third year medical student. We chatted about our weddings: she had gotten married that summer and I had been married for nearly four years.

She said, "You know my husband."

I replied, "I do?"

"Yes, you went to Northwestern together."

Lait.

Fast forward 20 years. I received a Facebook friend request from … Mr. Still as Lait as Ever (with a little more grey). He remembered me from medical school and knew I was a Northwestern alum.

A conversation ensued where he admitted hesitating to connect, given my hyphenated last name. We had both divorced. I decided to take this as an official move. On October 1, 2013, the fifth anniversary of the tragic day that changed my life forever, we eloped.

Five years ago, I couldn't see any beauty in my future. I could only see cancer, a heart defect, and my grief. So I saw ending my life prematurely as a logical solution. What a mistake in my thinking!

The mistake in my process was not keeping anyone around to talk me out of my despair. I needed someone to be close. I needed someone to have access to my heart. Fortunately, I had God while His help via people was on the way.

I didn't know my opportunity for a fresh start was coming, but it always was: the chance to break a bad habit or revive a lost dream, to get a handle on finances, to start a business, or to write a book. Had I not walked through the hard part, I would not have come to a place of celebration or perhaps of fulfilling my God ordained destiny. I decided not to waste another minute stuck in the past. I changed my mind, and I changed my life.

I did what I needed to do. It wasn't easy, and it took time, but my faith kept me on track. It took hard work and courage to choose recovery. It took hard work to change for continued growth. I had to look from the place where I was—and go!

There are moments in your life that make you and set the course of who you're going to be. Sometimes they're little, subtle moments. Sometimes, they're big moments you never saw coming. No one asks for their life to change, but it does. It's what you do afterwards that counts. That's when you find out who you are.

—Author unknown

These past few years have been my time to fly. I recall during the 2011 Susan G. Komen Seattle 3-Day, a gentleman said to me, "I don't know if anyone has told you, but I've been doing this for five years, and you are the best thing that could have happened to the 3-Day!" When someone gives me praise, I thank God and ask Him to keep me humble before Him. I have always wanted to be a blessing, and to do so on a national scale blows my mind.

In every city, after the event, I meet people in the airport who tell me how the event changed their lives and how I inspired them from beginning to end. I've been described as "magical," "awesome," and "amazing." One woman told me I was the glue that brought everything together. I was even told that I was the female James Earl Jones, and that listening to me was like listening to Maya Angelou. What if I had quit?

I've learned that I was not leaning on the Lord as He commanded in the Bible. If it wasn't prophesied to me, then somehow it wasn't so. He is meeting my needs and giving me the desires of my heart because the Word says He would. I wish my mom were alive to share in this experience with me, but her death has probably allowed me to live more in the moment and enjoy this time of blessing without the weight of her suffering. Mom's death taught me so much. Her life story ended where mine began, and her death added its signature.

I shared with a friend that when you have experienced death up close and personal and live through a diagnosis like cancer, your view of the world changes. He couldn't feel the way I did, though he did understand why I felt that way. Unless God says differently, the reality is that I will most likely die from cancer-related complications, and a cancer death is not an easy one. I live with this thought every day. It is not a pervasive thought, but one that causes me to live fervently and with purpose.

One man shared my vim. He shared his reasons for walking in all fourteen 3-Day events in 2013. At the top of his list was his beautiful wife of 30 years, Martha, who died from complications of breast cancer after a 20 year survivorship. I held up well through the first half of his presentation, then I completely lost it—like out of nowhere! One of those chest heaving, ugly cries ... In a split second, I had put myself in Martha's shoes.

Treatment as lengthy and as disruptive as mine has caused many survivors difficulty with returning to their normal daily life. A small number of survivors have become dependent on the attention and sympathy and feel neglected when life returns to normal.

Martha and I weren't in that number. As a matter of fact, we came out of treatment running to redeem any time stolen from us because of our disease. We insisted that life wasn't going to be business as usual, but better than before.

While survivors move forward one way or another, loved ones, i.e., co-survivors (particularly their partners) often experience tremendous impact from the cancer and treatment. They provide social support, which is critical in their long-term emotional adjustment.

Hearing John share his story from the perspective of a co-survivor caused me to reflect on my own co-survivors. I thought about the pain, fear, and uncertainty they must have felt and possibly still feel to this day. Some survivors, even if the cancer has been permanently cured, struggle emotionally from the trauma of having experienced a life-threatening disease. Our co-survivors struggle emotionally right along with us, maybe not to the degree or quite in the same way as we do. Their struggle is nonetheless very real. The diagnosis of a life-threatening illness for a family member creates fear of losing the loved one and concern about the suffering he or she will endure.

As John spoke, I remembered learning in medical school that chronic illness can bring about guilt, feelings of loss of control, anger, sadness, confusion, and fear, and I realized that I had experienced all of these. Both personally and professionally, I have seen survivors experience more generalized worry: fear for the future, an inability to make plans, uncertainty, and a heightened sense of vulnerability. When John said that Martha would force them to make plans and write them down every New Year's Day, I thought to myself, *Here was a woman after my own heart,* a woman who knew that when you put pen to paper, that is a step of creation, translating your desire into a physical reality.

As I listened to John, I heard his love, his pain, his adoration, his pride, and his loss. It was clear that he would always love Martha, though his heart was open to new beginnings. It was evident that their children loved, respected, and missed their mother. I guess when I lost it, I was thinking, *When it's my time to transcend from this life to the next, will I have someone who loves me like he loved her; will my children reflect my spirit, vision and zest for life; and will I leave behind a legacy worth remembering and telling others about?* His words confirmed that there is still work for me to do, that there are people in this world with buckets full of love ready to be dumped upon me daily, and that this is my time to explore, grow, and L.I.V.E. out all the possibilities that life has designed just for me.

As I tend to survivors, I try to always remember the people around them: their boss, their children, their friends, and their neighbors. All are important and in need of empathy. Both survivors and co-survivors need proactive support to reduce anxiety and depression, improve their mood, secure their self-image, practice coping skills, and stabilize their feelings when they feel out of control. My suffering has become an opportunity for blessing and abundance.

> The strength of a woman is not measured by the impact that all her hardships in life have had on her; the strength of a woman is measured by the extent of her refusal to allow those hardships to dictate her and who she becomes.
>
> —C. Joybell